Introduction to Attic Greek

ANSWER KEY

Introduction to Attic Greek

Second Edition

ANSWER KEY

Donald J. Mastronarde

UNIVERSITY OF CALIFORNIA PRESS
Berkeley · Los Angeles · London

University of California Press, one of the most distinguished university presses
in the United States, enriches lives around the world by advancing scholarship in
the humanities, social sciences, and natural sciences. Its activities are supported
by the UC Press Foundation and by philanthropic contributions from individuals
and institutions. For more information, visit www.ucpress.edu.

University of California Press
Berkeley and Los Angeles, California

University of California Press, Ltd.
London, England

ISBN 978-0-520-27574-4 (pbk., alk. paper)

Preface

This booklet provides the answers to the exercises appearing in the second edition of *Introduction to Attic Greek* by Donald J. Mastronarde (University of California Press, 2013). The Answer Key has been revised to match all the changes and additions made in the second edition.

Please note that in many of the exercises the answers given are not exhaustive of the possible correct answers. For instance, when an exercise asks the student to give one definition of the word, any one of the definitions supplied in the book is correct, but only one possible answer is indicated here. Similarly, sentences and passages to be translated from Greek to English may be correctly rendered with slightly different phrasing from what is given here. For Greek sentences composed by the student, there are of course many variations possible in word order and in treatment of details such as choice of conjunction for *and* or *but*, choice of synonym, and choice of equivalent constructions.

For most of the Greek-to-English sentences that were inspired by sentences in actual texts or taken unchanged or almost unchanged from an ancient text, a citation is provided.

When the first version of the Answer Key was prepared, Benjamin Acosta-Hughes checked the answers with great care. This time I have been assisted by Jeremy Simmons and copy editor Paul Psoinos. I alone am responsible for any errors or unclear answers that remain.

I. [NOTE: The references to §6 are optional parts of the answers.]

1. acute on *P*, *U* is long, §8 (short accented *P* has acute); §6 (acute may appear on *A*, *P*, or *U*)

2. circumflex on *P*, *U* is short, §8 (long accented *P* before short *U* has circumflex); §6 (circumflex may appear on *P* or *U*)

3. acute on *P*, *U* is long, §8 (long accented *P* before long *U* has acute); §6 (acute may appear on *A*, *P*, or *U*)

4. circumflex on *U*, *U* is long, §7 (long *U* may have circumflex); §6 (circumflex may appear on *P* or *U*)

5. circumflex on *U*, *U* is long, §7 (long *U* may have circumflex); §6 (circumflex may appear on *P* or *U*)

6. acute on *U*, *U* is long, §7; §6 (acute may appear on *A*, *P*, or *U*)

7. circumflex on *P*, *U* is short, §8 (long accented *P* before short *U* has circumflex); §6 (circumflex may appear on *P* or *U*); (second accent due to enclitic) additional acute on *U*, §12c

8. acute on *A*, *U* is short, §9 (accented *A* has acute, *U* must be short); §6 (acute may appear on *A*, *P*, or *U*); (second accent due to enclitic) additional acute on *U*, §12c

9. acute on *A*, *U* is short, §9 (accented *A* has acute, *U* must be short); §6 (acute may appear on *A*, *P*, or *U*)

10. acute on *U*, *U* is short, §7 (short accented *U* has acute in isolation); §6 (acute may appear on *A*, *P*, or *U*)

11. (first word) grave on *U*, *U* is short, §7 (short accented *U* has grave before another word); §6 (grave may appear only on *U*); (second word) acute on *U*, *U* is short, §7 (short accented *U* has acute in isolation); §6 (acute may appear on *A*, *P*, or *U*)

12. acute on *A*, *U* is short, §9 (accented *A* has acute, *U* must be short); §6 (acute may appear on *A*, *P*, or *U*)

13. (first word) grave on *U*, *U* is long, §7 (long accented *U* may have grave before another word); §6 (grave may appear only on *U*); (second word) acute on *A*, *U* is short, §9 (accented *A* has acute, *U* must be short); §6 (acute may appear on *A*, *P*, or *U*)

14. acute on *U*, *U* is short, §7 (short accented *U* has acute in isolation); §6 (acute may appear on *A*, *P*, or *U*)

15. circumflex on *U*, *U* is long, §7 (long *U* may have circumflex); §6 (circumflex may appear on *P* or *U*)

II.

1. δῶρᾰ
2. ἄνθρωπε
3. λαμβάνει
4. βούλεται
5. γλῶττᾰν
6. γλώττης
7. λόγον
8. λόγους
9. παιδείᾳ
10. ἄνεμος
11. ἀγαθόν
12. καλὸν δῶρον

UNIT THREE

I.

1. acc. sing. of ἥλιος, ἡλίου, m., *sun*
2. nom. *or* voc. pl. of πόλεμος, πολέμου, m., *war*
3. dat. pl. of βιβλίον, βιβλίου, n., *book*
4. gen. sing. of παιδίον, παιδίου, n., *child*
5. dat. sing. of θεός, θεοῦ, m. (or f.), *god* (or *goddess*)
6. nom. *or* voc. pl. of νόσος, νόσου, f., *sickness*
7. dat. sing. of ψῆφος, ψήφου, f., *pebble*
8. acc. pl. of θάνατος, θανάτου, m., *death*
9. acc. sing. of νόμος, νόμου, m., *law*
10. dat. pl. of ἄγγελος, ἀγγέλου, m., *messenger*
11. nom. *or* acc. *or* voc. pl. of μέτρον, μέτρου, n., *measure*
12. nom. *or* acc. *or* voc. pl. of δῶρον, δώρου, n., *gift*
13. gen. pl. of βίος, βίου, m., *life*
14. gen. pl. of ὁδός, ὁδοῦ, f., *road*
15. gen. sing. of ἵππος, ἵππου, m. (or f.), *horse* (or *mare*)
16. dat. sing. of ἄνθρωπος, ἀνθρώπου, m. or f., *human being*
17. acc. pl. of νόσος, νόσου, f., *sickness*
18. voc. sing. of ἄνεμος, ἀνέμου, m., *wind*
19. acc. sing. of λόγος, λόγου, m., *word*
20. dat. pl. of ἔργον, ἔργου, n., *work*

21. voc. sing. of ἀδελφός, ἀδελφοῦ, m., *brother*
22. gen. pl. of στρατηγός, στρατηγοῦ, m., *general*
23. dat. sing. of οἶκος, οἴκου, m., *house*
24. acc. sing. of στρατός, στρατοῦ, m., *army*

II.

1. ψῆφοι, f.
2. πολέμου, m.
3. παιδία, n.
4. νόσος, f.
5. μέτρον, n.
6. παιδία, n.
7. δῶρον, n.
8. ἥλιος, m.
9. θεοί, m. *or* f.
10. θανάτῳ, m.

11. ἔργοις, n.
12. ἀνθρώπων, m. *or* f.
13. ἵπποις, m. *or* f.
14. ὁδῷ, f.
15. λόγων, m.
16. ἀγγέλους, m.
17. βίε, m.
18. νόμου, m.
19. λόγος, m.
20. ἔργου, n.

21. ἀδελφοῖς, m.
22. στρατηγοί, m.
23. ἄνεμοι, m.
24. στρατοῦ, m.
25. οἴκους, m.
26. ἀγγέλοις, m.
27. παιδίῳ, n.
28. διδάσκαλον, m.

III.

1. even *or* also among men
2. to *or* into *or* with respect to sickness
3. in speech *or* word but not in deed
4. to *or* for a god and a human
5. from a horse
6. a general and not a messenger (subject)
7. even *or* also with teachers

8. out of war and death
9. in an army
10. to *or* for laws and votes
11. into a road but not into a house
12. with a wind
13. of life and death
14. out of fear *or* as a result of fear
15. of children and teachers

IV.

1. οὐ στρατηγοῖς ἀλλὰ στρατοῖς
2. εἰς φόβον καὶ θάνατον
3. καὶ σὺν ἀγγέλῳ
4. ἐν λόγοις καὶ (ἐν) νόμοις
5. οὐ δῶρον ἀλλὰ νόσον

6. ἀπ' ἀνθρώπων
7. ἐξ οἴκων
8. διδάσκαλοι καὶ νόμοι
9. καὶ ἐν ὁδῷ
10. εἰς ἀδελφούς

V.

1. πλοῦτον
2. χρόνοις
3. στρατηγέ
4. διδασκάλου

5. στρατοπέδοις
6. ἑταίρους
7. ποταμῷ
8. τρόπων

9. λίθοι
10. στάδια
11. υἱῶν
12. οὐρανοῦ

UNIT FOUR

I.

1. τὴν φιλίαν	12. τῇ νόσῳ	23. ταῖς ἀδελφαῖς
2. αἱ ἡδοναί	13. ἄνθρωπε	24. τῆς στρατιᾶς or τοῦ στρατοῦ
3. τῆς παιδείας	14. ταῖς ὁδοῖς	
4. τῶν φυγῶν	15. τῶν γνωμῶν	25. θεαί (or θεοί)
5. τῆς τιμῆς	16. τῇ φωνῇ	26. τὴν τιμήν
6. τὰς γνώμας	17. τὰς ἡμέρας	27. οἱ λόγοι
7. τῶν πολέμων	18. τὸ παιδίον	28. τῇ νίκῃ
8. ταῖς δίκαις	19. τὴν δίκην	29. τοὺς ἀνέμους
9. τὰς σκηνάς	20. αἱ ἡμέραι	30. τῶν θυρῶν
10. αἱ θύραι	21. τῆς ὁδοῦ	
11. ἀδελφαί	22. ψυχή	

II.

ἡ νόσος	τὰ δῶρα	ἡ νίκη	αἱ νίκαι
τῆς νόσου	τῶν δώρων	τῆς νίκης	τῶν νικῶν
τῇ νόσῳ	τοῖς δώροις	τῇ νίκῃ	ταῖς νίκαις
τὴν νόσον	τὰ δῶρα	τὴν νίκην	τὰς νίκας
(νόσε)	(δῶρα)	(νίκη)	(νῖκαι)

III.

1. dat. sing. of ψυχή, ψυχῆς, f., *soul*
2. acc. sing. of στρατιά, στρατιᾶς, f., *army*
3. nom. *or* voc. sing. of νίκη, νίκης, f., *victory*
4. dat. pl. of ἀγορά, ἀγορᾶς, f., *marketplace*
5. gen. pl. of τιμή, τιμῆς, f., *honor*
6. acc. pl. of ἀρετή, ἀρετῆς, f. *virtue*
7. nom. *or* voc. pl. of συμφορά, συμφορᾶς, f., *event*
8. gen. sing. *or* acc. pl. of θύρα, θύρας, f., *door*
9. acc. sing. of ἀρχή, ἀρχῆς, f., *beginning*
10. acc. pl. of θεά, θεᾶς, f., *goddess*
11. dat. pl. of δῶρον, δώρου, n., *gift*
12. dat. sing. of παιδεία, παιδείας, f., *education*
13. acc. pl. of λόγος, λόγου, m., *word*
14. nom. *or* acc. *or* voc. pl. of βιβλίον, βιβλίου, n., *book*
15. dat. sing. of τιμή, τιμῆς, f., *honor*

16. dat. pl. of *συμφορά, συμφορᾶς*, f., *event*
17. voc. sing. of *ἄγγελος, ἀγγέλου*, m., *messenger*
18. gen. pl. of *ἀγορά, ἀγορᾶς*, f., *marketplace*
19. acc. sing. of *θεός, θεοῦ*, m. (or f.), *god* (or *goddess*)
20. gen. sing. of *σκηνή, σκηνῆς*, f., *tent*
21. dat. sing. of *φωνή, φωνῆς*, f., *voice*
22. nom. *or* voc. pl. of *δίκη, δίκης*, f., *justice*
23. acc. pl. of *φυγή, φυγῆς*, f., *flight*
24. dat. pl. of *νίκη, νίκης*, f., *victory*
25. acc. sing. of *ἀδελφή, ἀδελφῆς*, f., *sister*
26. gen. sing. of *ἀρετή, ἀρετῆς*, f., *virtue*
27. nom. *or* voc. pl. of *ἡδονή, ἡδονῆς*, f., *pleasure*
28. gen. pl. of *ἀρχή, ἀρχῆς*, f., *beginning*
29. nom. *or* voc. pl. of *τιμή, τιμῆς*, f., *honor*
30. dat. pl. of *ἡμέρα, ἡμέρας*, f., *day*

IV.

1. The general brings the books too to Aspasia.
2. She *or* he takes the pebbles *or* votes.
3. The teacher leads the children out of the tent.
4. Children do not have judgment and virtue.
5. Xanthippe remains in the house with her sister *or* the sister, but her brother *or* the brother drives the horses into the road.
6. The army flees from the country.
7. War brings death and disease to *or* for mankind.
8. She *or* he has honor as a result of the victory.
9. She *or* he dissolves the democracy.
10. The messenger entrusts the children to the teachers.

V.

1. *σὺν (τῇ) ἡδονῇ*
2. *οὐ (τῆς) παιδείας ἀλλὰ (τῆς) φιλίας*
3. *νόμους γράφει καὶ τὴν δίκην εἰς τὴν χώραν φέρει.*
4. *καὶ εἰς τὴν ψυχήν*
5. *ὁ στρατηγὸς τοὺς θεοὺς καὶ τὰς θεὰς πείθει.*
6. *ἡ Ἀσπασία τὰ δῶρα τῷ ἀγγέλῳ ἐπιτρέπει.*
7. *ὁ στρατὸς* or *ἡ στρατιὰ οὐκ ἔχει φόβον καὶ ἐν τῇ ἀγορᾷ μένει.*

VI.

1. ἀνάγκην	5. εὐχῆς	9. ἡσυχίᾳ
2. μάχαις	6. σοφίαν	10. κεφαλῇ
3. ἐπιθυμίᾳ	7. πληγαί	11. δικαιοσύνην
4. εἰρηνῶν	8. ἐλευθερίας	12. σπουδῶν

UNIT FIVE

I.

1. πείθουσι(ν)	11. ἐθέλω	21. ἄρχετε
2. πέμπει	12. ἐθέλουσι(ν)	22. ἐπιτρέπει
3. λέγετε	13. ἐλαύνομεν	23. ἔχει
4. ἄρχουσι(ν)	14. γράφει	24. οὐ λαμβάνω
5. ἐπιτρέπω	15. ἄγουσι(ν)	25. λείπουσι(ν)
6. ἔχεις	16. ἐπιτρέπετε	26. λείπει
7. μένομεν	17. ἀποθνῄσκεις	27. ἐλαύνετε
8. λύει	18. οὐ πείθει	28. φεύγεις
9. ἄγει *or* φέρει	19. πέμπω	29. οὐ φέρομεν
10. λείπεις	20. λέγομεν	30. λέγει

II.

1. you (s.) are driving *or* marching
2. we bear
3. I write
4. he *or* she *or* it receives
5. they remain
6. you (s.) have
7. I urge *or* persuade
8. we are fleeing
9. he *or* she *or* it sends
10. we lead
11. I do not have
12. they are in exile *or* flee
13. you (s.) release
14. he *or* she *or* it bears
15. we entrust
16. you (pl.) do not send
17. they are leaving
18. I receive
19. you (s.) rule
20. he *or* she *or* it says
21. we release
22. I do not remain
23. you (pl.) are willing
24. they have
25. you (pl.) are driving *or* marching
26. I abandon
27. we begin
28. they are willing
29. you (pl.) hold office *or* begin
30. you (s.) say
31. he *or* she *or* it is abandoning
32. you (pl.) entrust

33. you (s.) remain
34. he *or* she *or* it is driving *or* marching
35. they are dying
36. I lead

37. we have
38. he *or* she *or* it is not leading
39. you (pl.) do not receive
40. you (s.) bear

III.

1. Peisistratus and Isaeus are persuading the generals but not the army.
2. We do not tell the story to the tyrant.
3. The goddess drives the sisters away from the house.
4. Are you dissolving *or* overthrowing the democracy?
5. From deeds and from speeches men have honor.
6. I am leading the horses out of the tent into the sun.
7. The general begins the war, and we have not victory but misfortunes.
8. Not justly *or* in justice do (the) tyrants write the laws.
9. The army leaves the marketplace and marches out of the country.

IV.

1. τὴν ἑταίραν εἰς τὴν οἶκον ἄγεις.
2. οἱ ἄνεμοι τοὺς ἑταίρους ἀπὸ τῆς χώρας φέρουσι(ν).
3. ἐκ τῆς νόσου οἱ ἵπποι ἀποθνῄσκουσι(ν).
4. (ἡ) Ἀσπασία φεύγει, ἀλλὰ δῶρα τοῖς παιδίοις πέμπει.
5. (ὁ) Ἰσαῖος καὶ (ἡ) Ξανθίππη πείθουσιν, ἀλλ᾽ οὐκ ἐθέλομεν.
6. τὸν διδάσκαλον λαμβάνετε, ἀλλὰ τὰ βιβλία μένει.

UNIT SIX

I.

1. πολίταις, m.
2. τραπεζῶν, f.
3. ἀλήθειαν, f.
4. μοῖραι, f.
5. δικαστοῦ, m.
6. κριτάς, m.
7. νεανίας, m.
8. δόξῃ, f.
9. ποιητά, m.
10. ναύτην, m.

11. δίκας, f.
12. ἑταίρων, m.
13. γνώμαις, f.
14. ὑγιείᾳ, f.
15. ναύτου, m.
16. τύραννον, m.
17. χῶραι, f.
18. βιβλία, n.
19. ὁπλῖτα, m.
20. θεαί, f.

21. γεφύρας, f.
22. δεσπόται, m.
23. τραπέζαις, f.
24. ὑγιείας, f.
25. ἀλήθεια, f.
26. νεανίαν, m.
27. ἱέρειαι, f.
28. πολίτῃ, m.
29. στρατιώτας, m.
30. γλωττῶν, f.

II.

1. nom. sing. of ὁπλίτης, ὁπλίτου, m., *hoplite*
2. acc. sing of ὑγίεια, ὑγιείας, f., *health*
3. dat. sing. of θάλαττα, θαλάττης, f., *sea*
4. acc. pl. of στρατιώτης, στρατιώτου, m., *soldier*
5. dat. pl. of χώρα, χώρας, f., *country*
6. gen. pl. of γλῶττα, γλώττης, f., *tongue*
7. nom. *or* voc. pl. of πεῖρα, πείρας, f., *attempt*
8. gen. sing. of ἀρχή, ἀρχῆς, f., *beginning*
9. dat. sing. of φωνή, φωνῆς, f., *voice*
10. acc. pl. of δόξα, δόξης, f., *reputation*
11. dat. sing. of γέφυρα, γεφύρας, f., *bridge*
12. nom. *or* voc. pl. of πολίτης, πολίτου, m., *citizen*
13. gen. sing. of δεσπότης, δεσπότου, m., *master*
14. gen. pl. of ναύτης, ναύτου, m., *sailor*
15. nom. *or* voc. pl. of φυγή, φυγῆς, f., *flight*
16. nom. *or* voc. pl. of στρατιώτης, στρατιώτου, m., *soldier*
17. voc. sing. of πολίτης, πολίτου, m., *citizen*
18. dat. sing. of ὑγίεια, ὑγιείας, f., *health*
19. acc. sing. of ἱέρεια, ἱερείας, f., *priestess*
20. acc. pl. of δεσπότης, δεσπότου, m., *master*
21. gen. sing. of δόξα, δόξης, f., *reputation*
22. dat. pl. of γλῶττα, γλώττης, f., *tongue*
23. acc. sing of ὁπλίτης, ὁπλίτου, m., *hoplite*
24. acc. sing of πεῖρα, πείρας, f., *attempt*
25. nom. *or* voc. pl. of ναύτης, ναύτου, m., *sailor*
26. gen. pl. of ἡδονή, ἡδονῆς, f., *pleasure*
27. acc. pl. of θάλαττα, θαλάττης, f., *sea*
28. gen. sing. of νόσος, νόσου, f., *sickness*
29. dat. pl. of τράπεζα, τραπέζης, f., *table*
30. gen. sing. of κριτής, κριτοῦ, m., *judge*
31. dat. sing. of ἀλήθεια, ἀληθείας, f., *truth*
32. gen. pl. of ἑταίρα, ἑταίρας, f., *courtesan*

III.

1. on account of the misfortunes
2. with fear
3. on behalf of the priestess *or* in front of the priestess
4. (ranking) after the young man
5. instead of the sun
6. in front of the tent *or* stage building
7. with (the) voice

8. throughout the day
9. thanks to *or* because of the courtesans
10. away from the sea
11. with the hoplites
12. after the attempt
13. as a result of (the) friendship
14. with the gifts
15. among the jurymen
16. with Callias
17. among the brothers
18. because of the sickness
19. with Xanthippe
20. into *or* in respect to the war

IV.

1. The gods do not persuade the Fates.
2. The comrades tell the truth to the umpire.
3. Because of the deeds we are releasing the messenger.
4. You (s.) are leading the sailors toward the sea.
5. The generals together with the *or* their soldiers are abandoning the tents and the mares.
6. The jurymen do not take gifts *or* bribes.
7. The master is entrusting the tables to the priestesses.
8. In the marketplace Callias is telling the citizens the victories.

V.

1. οἱ πολῖται νόμους ἔχουσιν ἀλλ᾽ οὐ δίκην.
2. ἐν τῷ πολέμῳ ἡ νόσος ἄρχει, καὶ οἱ ὁπλῖται φεύγουσι(ν).
3. οἱ ποιηταὶ διὰ τῆς γλώττης τοὺς πολίτας πείθουσι(ν).
4. οἱ στρατιῶται τὴν γέφυραν λαμβάνουσιν, ἀλλ᾽ ὁ στρατηγὸς ἀποθνῄσκει ἐν τῇ πείρᾳ.
5. δόξαν ἔχεις, ἀλλ᾽ οὐ λέγεις τὴν ἀλήθειαν.

UNIT SEVEN

I.

1. (τοῖς) αἰσχροῖς ἔργοις
2. τὴν χαλεπὴν συμφοράν
3. οἱ πονηροί
4. μέτρου δήλου
5. τῷ φιλίῳ ἀγγέλῳ
6. τοὺς πλουσίους κριτάς
7. γεφύρας καλῆς
8. ἀγαθῇ μοίρᾳ
9. τῶν ἱερῶν ὁδῶν
10. τὸν δίκαιον νόμον

II.

1. (a) in respect to the just account; (b) δίκαιον is acc. sing. masc. of δίκαιος, -α, -ον; (c) attributive modifying λόγου.

2. (a) through the large doors; (b) μακρῶν is gen. pl. fem. of μακρός, -ά, -όν; (c) attributive modifying θυρῶν.

3. (a) with the noble (*or* handsome *or* beautiful) gods (*or* goddesses); (b) καλῶν is gen. pl. masc. *or* fem. [depending on what the gender of θεῶν is taken to be] of καλός, -ή, -όν; (c) attributive modifying θεῶν.

4. (a) into the tent of the general; (b, c) no adjective form to identify.

5. (a) away from the enemy army; (b) πολεμίας is gen. sing. fem. of πολέμιος, -α, -ον; (c) attributive modifying στρατιᾶς.

6. (a) with the good (*or* well-born) men; (b) ἀγαθοῖς is dat. pl. masc. of ἀγαθός, -ή, -όν; (c) attributive modifying ἀνθρώποις.

7. (a) on account of the shamefulness (*or* ugliness); (b) αἰσχρόν is acc. sing. neuter of αἰσχρός, -ά, -όν; (c) used as a substantive.

8. (a) The children of Isaeus are small. (b) μικρὰ is nom. pl. neuter of μικρός, -ά, -όν; (c) predicative modifying παιδία.

9. (a) The just man is worthy of the office. (b) δίκαιος is nom. sing. masc. of δίκαιος, -α, -ον; (c) used as a substantive; (b) ἄξιος is nom. sing. masc. of ἄξιος, -α, -ον; (c) predicative modifying ὁ δίκαιος.

10. (a) Wicked men are deserving of evils *or* sufferings. (b) ἄξιοι is nom. pl. masc. of ἄξιος, -α, -ον; (c) predicative modifying οἱ πονηροί; (b) κακῶν is gen. pl. neuter of κακός, -ή, -όν; (c) used as a substantive; (b) πονηροί is nom. pl. masc. of πονηρός, -ά, -όν; (c) used as a substantive.

11. (a) Wise men speak the truth. (b) σοφοί is nom. pl. masc. of σοφός, -ή, -όν; (c) used as a substantive.

12. (a) The fate from the gods (*or* goddesses) is clear. (b) δήλη is nom. sing. fem. of δῆλος, -η, -ον; (c) predicative modifying μοῖρα.

13. (a) The books of the umpires are sacred. (b) ἱερὰ is nom. pl. neuter of ἱερός, -ά, -όν; (c) predicative modifying βιβλία.

14. (a) Because of the good deed the juror releases the bad man. (b) ἀγαθόν is acc. sing. neut. of ἀγαθός, -ή, -όν; (c) attributive modifying ἔργον; (b) κακόν is acc. sing. masc. of κακός, -ή, -όν; (c) used as substantive.

15. (a) The citizens are writing the laws with wise judgment. (b) σοφῆς is gen. sing. fem. of σοφός, -ή, -όν; (c) attributive with γνώμης.

16. (a) The sister is enduring the misfortunes of her brother with friendship (*or* loyalty) and pleasure. (b, c) no adjective form to identify.

III.

1. εἰς τὴν μικρὰν γέφυραν
2. διὰ τὴν τῶν πεζῶν ἀρετήν
3. ἐν τοῖς ἱεροῖς βιβλίοις
4. διὰ τοῦ μακροῦ βίου
5. σὺν τοῖς μικροῖς παιδίοις τοῖς τοῦ ἀγγέλου or μετὰ τῶν μικρῶν παιδίων τῶν τοῦ ἀγγέλου
6. ἡ τοῦ ποιητοῦ φυγὴ αἰσχρά.
7. τιμῆς ἄξια τὰ τῶν σοφῶν ἔργα.
8. τὰ ἀγαθὰ βιβλία φίλοι ἄξιοι.
9. οἱ ἐν τῇ ἀγορᾷ στρατιῶται καλοί.
10. οὐκ ἄγετε τὰ τοῦ ποιητοῦ παιδία ἐκ τῆς μακρᾶς σκηνῆς.
11. τοὺς πλουσίους λαμβάνομεν καὶ οὐ τοὺς δικαίους πολίτας.

UNIT EIGHT

I.

1. away from the sea (that lies) beside the country
2. in charge of the slave women
3. against the soldiers in the house
4. after the slaves' attempt
5. because of the noble habits
6. from the jurymen
7. in the time of Peisistratus
8. from (the presence *or* the side) of the general of the enemies
9. on account of the envy against the wise men
10. in addition to the gifts
11. toward the sun
12. from the friends
13. in the river
14. toward the road
15. upon the tables
16. alongside the road to the shrine
17. in addition to wealth
18. out of sleep
19. at the side of (*or* in the house of) the bad teacher

II.

1. διὰ τὸν πόνον
2. παρὰ τοῖς παιδίοις
3. πρὸς (or ἐπὶ) ταῖς τῆς ἑταίρας θύραις
4. παρὰ (or πρὸς or ἀπὸ) τῶν πολιτῶν
5. μετὰ τὴν νίκην
6. πρὸς τὰς Μοίρας
7. πρὸς (or ἐπὶ) τῇ τραπέζῃ
8. ἐπὶ τῶν μικρῶν ἵππων
9. παρὰ τὴν τοῦ ἀγγέλου δόξαν
10. ἐκ τοῦ καλοῦ ποταμοῦ
11. ἐπὶ Ἰσαίου
12. πρὸς (or ἐπὶ) τοὺς ἀγαθοὺς νεανίας

III.

1. The god sends a panic and drives the soldiers out of the shrine.
2. Mankind has its sufferings from the gods. [In a particular context, θεῶν could be "goddesses" from θεά; but in a generic statement without context the generic masculine would be idiomatically assumed.]
3. Young men, carry the gifts to *or* for the worthy men.
4. Leave [sing. addressee] the enemies' horses next to the bridge.
5. The messengers are telling the misfortunes of the army to the citizens (who are) in the marketplace.
6. The brother, who is in exile from his land for a long time, receives his livelihood (*or* sustenance) from his friends.
7. The slave woman to whom you (pl.) are entrusting the health of the children is wise and friendly.
8. The hoplite, who endures difficult things and avoids shameful things, does not abandon his comrades.
9. Citizens, do not begin a war, but in war do not have fear.

IV.

1. αἰσχροὶ οἱ λόγοι δι' ὧν τοὺς πολίτας πείθεις.
2. ὁ δεσπότης τοὺς δούλους εἰς τὴν ἱέρειαν πέμπει, καὶ τὰ παιδία τὰ ἱερὰ ἐκ τῆς σκηνῆς φέρει.
3. ποιητά, μὴ φθόνον ἔχε.
4. Ἰσαῖε, γράφε δικαίους νόμους τοῖς τῆς χώρας πολίταις.
5. μὴ λέγε (τὰ) αἰσχρά, ἀλλ' ἃ εἰς ἀρετὴν ἄγει τοὺς ἀνθρώπους.
6. ἡ ὁδὸς ἡ ἀπὸ τοῦ ἱεροῦ εἰς (or πρὸς) τὸν ποταμὸν μακρὰ καὶ χαλεπή.

UNIT NINE

I.

1. ἄγειν	5. ἐκ τοῦ λέγειν	9. ἄρχει
2. κελεύετε	6. ἀκούουσι(ν)	10. ἐλαύνω
3. οὐ βλάπτομεν	7. λύειν	11. ἀκούετε
4. τάττειν	8. πείθειν	12. τάττε

II.

1. Urge the army to remain. *or* You (pl.) are urging the army to remain.
2. The sailor orders the soldiers to abandon their mares.
3. He *or* she is willing to entrust the difficult tasks to the handsome young men.
4. I do not wish to die in the sea.

5. You (s.) are ordering the hoplites not to harm the rich citizens. [This could also mean: "You are ordering the rich citizens not to harm the hoplites." There is no way to decide which meaning is preferable except by the context, and in the absence of context, as here, by general likelihood.]

6. The god is unwilling to listen to the goddess who says bad things.

7. It seems best to the wise to speak the truth. [Not impossible: "It seems best to speak the truth to the wise."]

8. It is necessary (*or* one ought *or* we ought) to drive the impious ones away from the tent of the children. [Not impossible: "It is necessary for the impious ones to march *or* ride away from the children's tent."]

9. The allies are commanding the foreigners to take the marketplace.

10. The immortals urge human beings not so say impious things.

11. Because of the fact that the enemy are remaining in the country the citizens are fleeing toward the sea.

12. It is easy for good men to write laws. [Not impossible: "It is easy to write laws for good people."]

13. It is necessary for the sailors to await a fair wind. *or* The sailors ought to await a fair wind.

14. It is possible for *or* permitted to the generals to harm the enemy.

III.

1. μετὰ τῶν φίλων ῥᾴδιον κακὰ φέρειν.

2. ὁ τῆς πολεμίας στρατιᾶς στρατηγὸς τοὺς ὁπλίτας τάττει.

3. τὰ παιδία τὸν τύραννον τὴν μοῖραν τοῖς θεοῖς ἐπιτρέπειν πείθει.

4. τοῖς ἀθανάτοις θεοῖς οὐκ ἔξεστι φθόνον ἔχειν.

5. ἔξεστι τῷ πονηρῷ (or κακῷ) μὴ κακὴν δόξαν ἔχειν (or κακὴν δόξαν μὴ ἔχειν).

6. οὐ σοφὸν τὴν ὑγίειαν βλάπτειν.

7. διὰ τὸν πλοῦτον ἔξεστι τοῖς πλουσίοις τὰ χαλεπὰ (ἔργα) φεύγειν.

8. τὸν ποιητὴν χρὴ μὴ ἐθέλειν κακὰ λέγειν.

9. πρὸς τῇ τιμῇ τὸ ἄρχειν (τὸν) φθόνον φέρει.

10. ὦ δικασταί, ἀκούετε τοῦ δικαίου καὶ μὴ τοῦ ἀδίκου.

UNIT TEN

I.

1. They are immortal.

2. You (pl. [masc. *or* generic]) are not brave *or* good.

3. It is unjust.

4. I am a friend.

5. It is clear.

6. You (s. [masc.]) are wicked.
7. We are not wise.
8. She is wise.
9. It is difficult.

10. Be pious (pl. fem. addressees).
11. It is not a stone.
12. The beautiful exists.

II.

1. ἄξιόν ἐστι(ν).
2. αἴτιοί εἰσιν οἱ Ἀθηναῖοι. or
   οἱ Ἀθηναῖοι αἴτιοί εἰσιν, or
   οἱ Ἀθηναῖοί εἰσιν αἴτιοι. or
   αἴτιοι οἱ Ἀθηναῖοί εἰσιν.
3. ἡ μάχη ἐστὶ μακρά. or
   ἡ μάχη μακρά ἐστι. or
   μακρά ἐστιν ἡ μάχη. or
   μακρὰ ἡ μάχη ἐστίν.
4. ἀθάνατοί ἐσμεν.
5. ναύτης εἰμί.
6. ὅσιος εἶ. or ὁσία εἶ. or εἶ ὅσιος. or εἶ
   ὁσία.
7. δίκαιοί ἐστε. or δίκαιαί ἐστε.

8. ἡ ἐπιορκία οὐ δικαία ἐστίν. or
   οὐκ ἔστι δικαία ἡ ἐπιορκία. or
   ἡ ἐπιορκία ἐστὶν οὐ δικαία. or
   οὐ δικαία ἡ ἐπιορκία ἐστί. or
   οὐ δικαία ἐστὶν ἡ ἐπιορκία. or
   ἡ ἐπιορκία οὐκ ἔστι δικαία.
9. αἰτία ἐστίν.
10. μικρά ἐστιν ἡ ψῆφος. or
    ἡ ψῆφός ἐστι μικρά. or
    μικρά ἡ ψῆφός ἐστιν. or
    ἡ ψῆφος μικρά ἐστιν.
11. ὁ τύραννός ἐστιν ὁ στρατηγός. or
    ὁ τύραννος ὁ στρατηγός ἐστιν.

III.

1. (a) The majority of the citizens are just. (b) genitive, partitive
2. (a) For (*or* in the eyes of) the wicked man the laws are not fine. (b) dative of reference
3. (a) The desire for wealth persuades human beings to suffer evils. (b) genitive, objective
4. (a) On the following day they write a peace treaty. (b) dative of time when
5. (a) The immortals are responsible for good things for mankind. (b) genitive, objective with αἴτιος
6. (a) The victory belongs to the Athenians. (b) genitive of possession
7. (a) The impious men are taking small stones from the river with which they are pelting the shrine. (b) dative of means or instrument
8. (a) There is no need to mention the enemy's fear. (b) genitive, subjective
9. (a) Do fine things and avoid unjust deeds. (b) accusative, direct object
10. (a) In the previous battle most of the hoplites do not flee. (b) nominative, subject

IV.

1. χαλεποῖς πόνοις οἱ σύμμαχοι τὴν ἀγορὰν λαμβάνουσιν.
2. χρὴ (or δεῖ) τοὺς ἀνθρώπους (τὰ) δίκαια πράττειν.
3. μετὰ τὴν μάχην οἱ στρατιῶται εἰς τὴν τῶν Ἀθηναίων χώραν φεύγουσιν.
4. ἡ ἐπιθυμία τῆς εἰρήνης τοὺς πολίτας πείθει μὴ βλάπτειν τοὺς τῶν πολεμίων ἀγγέλους.
5. οἱ δικασταὶ τὰ πλεῖστα τῶν ἀδίκων ἔργων εὑρίσκουσιν, ἀνθ᾽ ὧν τοὺς αἰτίους βλάπτουσιν.
6. τῶν σοφῶν ἐστι τὰς καλὰς ἡδονὰς εὑρίσκειν.
7. τοὺς πολίτας ἀνάγκη (or δεῖ or χρὴ) πάσχειν διὰ τὸν πρὸς τοὺς βαρβάρους πόλεμον.
8. τῷ ἀγαθῷ οὐ πρέπει ἀδίκῳ εἶναι.
9. τοῖς πλείστοις ἡ ἡδονὴ οὐκ ἔστι τὸ μέτρον τῆς ἀρετῆς.

UNIT ELEVEN

I.

1. 1 pl. pres. act. ind. of σπένδω, *we are pouring libations*
2. 2 s. pres. m./p. ind. of μάχομαι, *you (s.) are fighting*
3. 2 pl. pres. m./p. ind. of κόπτω, *you (pl.) are beating your breast* [i.e., in mourning] OR *you are being beaten;* OR 2 pl. pres. m./p. impt. of κόπτω, *beat your breast* [i.e., in mourning] (pl.) OR *be beaten* (pl.)
4. 3 pl. pres. m./p. ind. of γράφω, *they are indicting* or *they are being drawn* or *written*
5. 2 s. pres. act. ind. of λαμβάνω, *you (s.) are taking*
6. 3 s. pres. m./p. ind. of γίγνομαι, *she* or *he is being born* or *it is happening*
7. pres. act. inf. of πράττω, *to do*
8. 1 s. pres. m./p. ind. of βουλεύω, *I am deliberating*
9. 3 pl. pres. m./p. ind. of ἔρχομαι, *they are going*
10. 2 s. pres. m./p. ind. of ἔχω, *you (s.) cling to* or *you (s.) are being held*
11. 3 s. pres. m./p. ind. of λέγω, *it is being said* or *it is said*
12. 2 pl. pres. m./p. ind. of οἴομαι, *you (pl.) believe* OR 2 pl. pres. m./p. impt. of οἴομαι, *believe* (pl.)
13. 2 pl. pres. act. ind. of πάσχω, *you (pl.) suffer* OR 2 pl. pres. act. impt. of πάσχω, *suffer* (pl.)
14. 3 pl. pres. act. ind. of εἰμί, *they are*
15. pres. m./p. inf. of πολιτεύω, *to participate in politics*
16. 3 s. pres. m./p. ind. of βούλομαι, *she* or *he wants*

17. 3 pl. pres. act. ind. of δικάζω, *they serve as jurors*
18. 1 pl. pres. m./p. ind. of σπένδω, *we are making a truce*
19. 2 s. pres. act. impt. of ἀποκτείνω, *kill* (s.)
20. 2 s. pres. m./p. ind. of αἰσθάνομαι, *you* (s.) *perceive*
21. 2 s. pres. m./p. impt. of ἔχω, *cling to* (s.)
22. 2 pl. pres. act. ind. of βλάπτω, *you* (pl.) *are harming* OR 2 pl. pres. act. impt. of βλάπτω, *harm* (pl.)
23. 3 s. pres. m./p. ind. of βάλλω, *it is being thrown* or *she* or *he* or *it is being pelted*
24. 2 s. pres. m./p. ind. of ἄγω, *you* (s.) *are being led*
25. 2 pl. pres. m./p. ind. of παρακελεύομαι, *you* (pl.) *are exhorting* OR 2 pl. pres. m./p. impt. of παρακελεύομαι, *exhort* (pl.)
26. 3 pl. pres. m./p. ind. of πυνθάνομαι, *they are inquiring*
27. 3 s. pres. m./p. ind. of δικάζω, *she* or *he pleads a case*
28. 1 pl. pres. act. ind. of ἀκούω, *we hear*
29. 3 s. pres. m./p. ind. of λείπω, *she* or *he* or *it is being left*
30. 2 s. pres. m./p. impt. of γίγνομαι, *become* (s.)

II.

1. ἐρχόμεθα
2. δικάζει
3. ἔχεσθε
4. βούλονται
5. παρασκευάζου
6. δικάζεται
7. σπένδουσι(ν)
8. βουλεύεσθε
9. παρακελεύῃ
10. πυνθανόμεθα
11. λύεται
12. πυνθάνονται or ἀκούουσι(ν)
13. τάττεσθε
14. γυμνάζεσθαι
15. πολιτεύομαι
16. μάχονται
17. οἴῃ
18. ἄγεται
19. γραφόμεθα
20. γίγνονται
21. ἀρχόμεθα
22. πυνθάνεσθαι
23. οὐκ ἐθέλω
24. παρασκευάζειν
25. οἴεται
26. ἐσμέν
27. εἶναι
28. κόπτεται
29. φέρεσθαι or ἄγεσθαι
30. εὑρίσκεσθε

III.

1. In the war against the foreigners (*or* the Persians) the Athenians are fighting against brave enemies.
2. Generals must deliberate.
3. They command the hoplites to position themselves (*or* be positioned) alongside the river.
4. Do not make a truce, but desire to fight.
5. By means of difficult toils victory comes about for the Athenians. *or* By means of difficult toils the Athenians get a victory.

6. They make a truce on the following day.
7. One must cling to one's honor.
8. You are being harmed not by the enemy but by the soldiers who exhort (you) to flee.
9. It is not possible for (the) children to pour libations to the gods.
10. The sailors are being driven by the winds toward the land of the foreigners.
11. Hear the arguments *or* speeches, Athenians, and deliberate.
12. Fight, young man, beside your comrades, and win victory for yourself.
13. Most of the soldiers are unwilling to flee.
14. The children are being led into *or* toward the shrine by their teacher.
15. Be worthy of the office that the citizen entrust (to you).
16. It seems best to Isaeus to marry the sister of the poet.

UNIT TWELVE

I.

1. in front of the tents
2. under the power (*or* control) of the impious master
3. in accordance with the judgment of the judge
4. concerning the honor of the Athenians
5. on behalf of the same friends
6. under the power (*or* control) of the enemy
7. (up) along the road
8. throughout the previous day
9. in return for her toils
10. across (*or* over) the sea
11. under (*or* into) the tent
12. around the marketplace
13. against the umpires
14. before the battle itself
15. toward *or* against the foreigners
16. about (*or* over) victory
17. in accordance with the just account
18. by those in the shrine

II.

1. The wise fare well; the bad do not.
2. We want to have not war but peace.
3. The citizens pour libations to the gods who fight on behalf of the country. For they are responsible for (its *or* their) faring well.
4. The land across the river into which his children are going is beautiful.
5. By both the Athenians themselves and their allies the foreigners are now justly being harmed.
6. To do just things is difficult for most people but easy for the wise.
7. She *or* he exhorts the citizens to be pious both now and in the future.

8. Good men always want to have honor instead of wealth.

9. Peisistratus is now arranging the foot soldiers here beside the sea, while Isaeus and the sailors are easily going up the river. For it seems best to them to leave the army now *or* immediately.

10. The priestess is entrusting the majority of the slaves to her brother; but they immediately want to flee, for they are in a bad way.

11. The teacher orders the young men to bear their toils well, but they are not willing to obey him.

III.

1. σοφῶς, αἰσχρῶς, κακῶς, χαλεπῶς, ἀδίκως

2. ὑπὲρ or πρὸ αὐτῶν τῶν τυράννων (or τῶν τυράννων αὐτῶν)

3. κατὰ τοὺς τῶν βαρβάρων νόμους

4. περὶ τῆς δημοκρατίας or περὶ τὴν δημοκρατίαν

5. οἱ ὁπλῖται οἷς τὰ παιδία ἐπιτρέπομεν καὶ δίκαιοί εἰσι καὶ ὅσιοι (or καὶ δίκαιοι καὶ ὅσιοι).

6. ὁ μὲν τὴν ἀλήθειαν λέγει, ὁ δὲ οὔ.

7. ἀνὰ τὸν ποταμὸν χαλεπῶς ἔρχονται οἱ ναῦται· λίθοις γὰρ ὑπὸ τῶν πολεμίων βάλλονται.

8. αἱ ἵπποι περὶ ὧν λέγετε οὐκ αὐτῶν τῶν ἱερειῶν εἰσιν ἀλλὰ τῶν θεῶν.

9. ἀεὶ χρὴ μάλα σοφῶς βουλεύεσθαι ὑπὲρ τῶν πολιτῶν.

10. οὐ ῥᾴδιον (or οὐ ῥᾴδιόν ἐστιν) αὐτοῖς χαλεπῷ νόμῳ πείθεσθαι.

11. τοὺς περὶ τῶν συμμάχων λόγους αὖθις or αὖ ἀκούομεν. ἔπειτα or εἶτα τοῦ πολέμου ἄρχομεν.

UNIT THIRTEEN

I.

1. δοκοῦμεν	12. φοβοῦσι(ν)	22. ἄγονται
2. φοβοῦνται	13. ποιεῖται	23. ἀφικνοῦνται
3. ὠφελεῖς	14. δοκεῖν	24. δεῖσθαι
4. ἀφικνεῖται	15. ὠφελούμεθα	25. ποιοῦμεν
5. φιλεῖ	16. κελεύουσι(ν)	26. γράφῃ
6. φίλει	17. κρατῶ	27. αἱρῇ
7. οἰκεῖται	18. βλάπτεσθαι or	28. δοκεῖ
8. βουλόμεθα	ἀδικεῖσθαι	29. ὠφελῶ
9. νοσοῦσι(ν)	19. γίγνῃ	30. φοβούμεθα
10. σπένδεσθε	20. αἱρεῖτε	
11. φοβεῖσθαι	21. ἀδικεῖται	

II.

1. you (pl.) are ill *or* [unlikely] be ill (pl.)   2 pl. pres. act. ind. [*or* impt.] of νοσέω
2. they ask for   3 pl. pres. m./p. ind. of δέομαι
3. to seem   pres. act. inf. of δοκέω
4. I am liked   1 s. pres. m./p. ind. of φιλέω
5. we seize   1 pl. pres. act. ind. of αἱρέω
6. she *or* he *or* it helps   3 s. pres. act. ind. of ὠφελέω
7. to arrive   pres. m./p. inf. of ἀφικνέομαι
8. you (s.) are being conquered   2 s. pres. m./p. ind. of κρατέω
9. they seem   3 pl. pres. act. ind. of δοκέω
10. I dwell   1 s. pres. act. ind. of οἰκέω
11. you (pl.) are being wronged *or* [unlikely] be wronged (pl.)   2 pl. pres. m./p. ind. of ἀδικέω / 2 pl. pres. m./p. impt. of ἀδικέω
12. she *or* he arrives   3 s. pres. m./p. ind. of ἀφικνέομαι
13. to terrify   pres. act. inf. of φοβέω
14. you (s.) make   2 s. pres. act. ind. of ποιέω
15. we are afraid   1 pl. pres. m./p. ind. of φοβέω
16. she *or* he inquires   3 s. pres. m./p. ind. of πυνθάνομαι
17. you (s.) hear   2 s. pres. act. ind. of ἀκούω
18. you (s.) find for yourself *or* you (s.) are being discovered   2 s. pres. m./p. ind. of εὑρίσκω
19. to do wrong   pres. act. inf. of ἀδικέω
20. it is necessary   3 s. pres. act. ind. of δέω *or* δεῖ
21. they conquer   3 pl. pres. act. ind. of κρατέω
22. they are being inhabited   3 pl. pres. m./p. ind. of οἰκέω
23. we choose *or* we are being seized   1 pl. pres. m./p. ind. of αἱρέω
24. you (pl.) love *or* love (pl.)   2 pl. pres. act. ind. *or* impt. of φιλέω
25. you (s.) engage in politics   2 s. pres. m./p. ind. of πολιτεύω
26. help (s.)   2 s. pres. act. impt. of ὠφελέω
27. it is being made *or* she *or* he makes for herself *or* himself   3 s. pres. m./p. ind. of ποιέω
28. you (s.) seem   2 s. pres. act. ind. of δοκέω
29. I am being aided   1 s. pres. m./p. ind. of ὠφελέω
30. we are becoming   1 pl. pres. m./p. ind. of γίγνομαι

III.

1. τούσδε τοὺς ἀγαθοὺς Ἀθηναίους
2. ἐκείνῳ τῷ πονηρῷ συμμάχῳ
3. ἥδε (or αὕτη) ἡ καλὴ νίκη
4. τούτων (or τῶνδε) τῶν χαλεπῶν πόνων
5. ἐκεῖνα τὰ φίλα παιδία
6. ἐκείνη ἡ κακὴ δόξα
7. τούτους (or τούσδε) τοὺς πλουσίους
8. ταύτῃ (or τῇδε) τῇ πολεμίᾳ στρατιᾷ or τούτῳ (or τῷδε) τῷ πολεμίῳ στρατῷ
9. ἐκείνων τῶν κακῶν συμφορῶν
10. ἐκεῖνο τὸ σοφὸν ἔργον

IV.

1. The foreigners whom those men are conquering dwell by the sea.
2. These women terrify the children; those are afraid of them.
3. On this day it seems best to the citizens to make peace with the enemy, for most of the soldiers are sick.
4. Those people do wrong to the good but help the bad.
5. The wise general has need of the following, I suppose: deliberating well before the battle and faring well in the battle.
6. This man easily wins honor for himself; so just and wise does he seem to the citizens because of the fine laws that he writes.
7. The sailors who arrive here always seem to aid the foreigners *or* the Persians.
8. While these brothers dwell in the same house, their sisters dwell in the shrine with the priestesses.
9. Do not choose in life the easy (things) but the noble. *or* Choose in life not the easy but the noble.
10. We beseech also the Athenians not shamefully to desert the Greeks there.

V.

1. καὶ αὕτη ἡ χώρα ὑπό τε τῶν βαρβάρων καὶ ὑπὸ τῶν Ἀθηναίων οἰκεῖται.
2. διὰ τὴν προτέραν εἰρήνην οὐκ ἔξεστι τῷ στρατηγῷ τοὺς ἐν τῷ τῆς θεᾶς ἱερῷ ὠφελεῖν.
3. οἱ κακοὶ τῶν πλείστων ἄρχουσιν· οἱ γὰρ ἀγαθοὶ νῦν ἄρχειν οὐκ ἐθέλουσιν.
4. ἐκ τοῦ ἀδικεῖν ἀλλὰ ἀγαθὸς δοκεῖν (εἶναι), ὁ ἄδικος τὸν πλοῦτον καὶ τὴν τιμὴν φέρεται· οἱ γὰρ πολῖται αὐτὸν μάλα φιλοῦσιν.
5. τῶν νεανιῶν οἱ μὲν νῦν ἀφικνοῦνται, οἱ δὲ ἤδη γυμνάζονται.
6. μὴ οὕτω or ὧδε φοβοῦ or φοβεῖσθε τοὺς ἀνέμους καὶ τὴν θάλατταν.

UNIT FOURTEEN

I.

1. χάρι	11. γιγάντων	21. θώρακι
2. γέρουσι(ν)	12. κλῶπες	22. ὄρνιν
3. ὕδωρ	13. πρᾶγμα	23. γίγαν
4. ποιημάτων	14. Ἑλλάδι	24. γράμμασι(ν)
5. λέοντες	15. φύλαξι(ν)	25. φῶς
6. ὀδόντι	16. ἀσπίδος	26. ὑδάτων
7. ἐλπίδες	17. πατρίδας	27. ὄρνιθες
8. φάλαγγος	18. τέρατα	28. χάριτι
9. ὄρνιθι	19. γράμμα	29. φύλακες
10. ἔριδας	20. βουλευμάτων	30. φυγάδος

II.

1. gen. pl. of θώραξ, θώρακος, f.
2. dat. pl. of λέων, λέοντος, m.
3. dat. sing. of φῶς, φωτός, n.
4. acc. pl. of ὀδούς, ὀδόντος, m.
5. nom. *or* acc. *or* voc. pl. of βούλευμα, βουλεύματος, n.
6. gen. sing. of φάλαγξ, φάλαγγος, f.
7. acc. sing. of ἐλπίς, ἐλπίδος, f.
8. nom. *or* voc. pl. of ὄρνις, ὄρνιθος, m. *or* f.
9. dat. sing. of φύλαξ, φύλακος, m.
10. gen. sing. of ἔρις, ἔριδος, f.
11. nom. sing. of πατρίς, πατρίδος, f.
12. dat. pl. of ἀσπίς, ἀσπίδος, f.
13. nom. *or* voc. pl. of κλώψ, κλωπός, m.
14. dat. pl. of ποίημα, ποιήματος, n.
15. nom. *or* acc. *or* voc. sing. of πρᾶγμα, πράγματος, n.
16. acc. sing. of χάρις, χάριτος, f.
17. acc. sing. of Ἑλλάς, Ἑλλάδος, f.
18. dat. pl. of φυγάς, φυγάδος, m. *or* f.
19. gen. pl. of ὕδωρ, ὕδατος, n.
20. acc. pl. of γίγας, γίγαντος, m.
21. gen. pl. of γέρων, γέροντος, m.
22. dat. pl. of ὀδούς, ὀδόντος, m.
23. gen. sing. of φῶς, φωτός, n.
24. dat. sing. of ὕδωρ, ὕδατος, n.

III.

1. Because of the good omens we are not afraid of the war against those people.
2. It is bad to abandon one's shield but good to save one's life.
3. After this [literally, *these things*] the old men carry water to the young men who are fighting on behalf of the fatherland.
4. The sentinels whom the enemy capture are put to death.
5. Heracles must defeat both the lion in Nemea and the giants and the monsters throughout Greece.

6. Health is a good thing for human beings, but it is bad to feel ill *or* be in bad shape.

7. Worthy poems are not written by bad *or* wretched poets.

8. In wartime we want to hear the portents that the gods seem to send, but in peacetime we do not.

9. The sister of the exile does not remain in the house but is always beside the doors. And then the tyrant seizes her but is afraid to put her to death.

IV.

1. τοῖς πολίταις δοκεῖ τοῦτον τὸν ποιητὴν αἱρεῖσθαι· οὐ γὰρ φιλοῦσι τοὺς πλείστους αὐτῶν.

2. ἐκείνου δεῖται ὑπὲρ τῆς εἰρήνης λέγειν.

3. ταῦτα οὐχ οὕτως or ὧδε ἔχει, ἀλλ᾽ ἀεὶ εὖ or καλῶς πράττετε.

4. χάριν οὐκ ἔχουσι τῷ Πεισιστράτῳ τῶν ἀγαθῶν ἃ ποιεῖ or πράττει;

UNIT FIFTEEN

I.

1. dat. sing. of ἔτος, ἔτους, n.

2. gen. sing. of Σωκράτης, Σωκράτους, m.

3. nom. *or* acc. *or* voc. pl. of τεῖχος, τείχους, n.

4. gen. sing. of πατήρ, πατρός, m.

5. dat. sing. of Ἕλλην, Ἕλληνος, m.

6. gen. pl. of δαίμων, δαίμονος, m. *or* f.

7. dat. pl. of ῥήτωρ, ῥήτορος, m.

8. acc. pl. of μήτηρ, μητρός, f.

9. voc. sing. of θυγάτηρ, θυγατρός, f.

10. nom. *or* acc. *or* voc. pl. of κράτος, κράτους, n.

11. gen. pl. of μέρος, μέρους, n.

12. dat. sing. of γῆρας, γήρως, n.

13. dat. pl. of τριήρης, τριήρους, f.

14. dat. sing. of ἀνήρ, ἀνδρός, m.

15. acc. sing. of ἅλς, ἁλός, m. *or* f.

16. acc. sing. of ἀγών, ἀγῶνος, m.

17. voc. sing. of Δημοσθένης, Δημοσθένους, m.

18. nom. *or* acc. *or* voc. pl. of γέρας, γέρως, n.

19. gen. sing. of πλῆθος, πλήθους, n.

20. nom. *or* acc. *or* voc. sing. of τέλος, τέλους, n.

21. gen. pl. masc. *or* fem. *or* neuter of τίς, τί

22. acc. pl. of ἀνήρ, ἀνδρός, m.

23. voc. sing. of πατήρ, πατρός, m.

24. acc. sing. of τριήρης, τριήρους, f.

25. gen. sing. of γῆρας, γήρως, n.

26. acc. sing. masc. *or* fem. *or* nom. *or* acc. pl. neuter of τίς, τί

27. dat. sing. of κράτος, κράτους, n.

28. nom. *or* voc. pl. of δαίμων, δαίμονος, m. *or* f.

29. dat. pl. of ἀγών, ἀγῶνος, m.

30. dat. pl. masc. *or* fem. *or* neuter of τίς, τί

II.

1. τί μέρος; or τίς μοῖρα;
2. τοῖς ἀδίκοις ῥήτροσι(ν)
3. τὰς πλείστας τῶν τριήρων
4. τίνων Ἑλλήνων;
5. γέρως μικροῦ
6. κακὴν ἔριν
7. μακροὶ ὀδόντες
8. κατὰ (ὑπὸ) ἐκεῖνο τὸ ἔτος
9. τῷ σοφῷ βουλεύματι
10. τίνες ἐλπίδες;
11. τοῦδε (τούτου) τοῦ πλήθους
12. μετὰ τὸν ἀγῶνα
13. τίσι μητράσι(ν);
14. πρὸς τὸ τεῖχος ἐκεῖνο
15. σὺν τῷ ἀνδρί or μετὰ τοῦ ἀνδρός

III.

1. Who is the speaker? Demosthenes, who urges the multitude to entrust the triremes to the rich and to pay in taxes.
2. What should one do? For some of the Greeks are afraid to fight in the land of the Persians, and others are unwilling to obey the general of the Athenians.
3. The father and the mother love their daughter and are loved by her.
4. Which contest are the umpires preparing? Which young men are winning prizes?
5. It is impious not to have (feel) gratitude for the good deeds which those men are doing on behalf of the democracy.
6. Exhort the messenger to send the hoplites immediately and lead them to the long walls.
7. Do this yourself on behalf of your father, but do not wrong his friends.
8. The goddess Strife is treated unjustly by the immortals. For they do not want this (goddess) to be with the other gods, who are friendly to Peleus. For they command him to marry Thetis. And because of this, Strife becomes responsible for the fact that very many of the fine and noble men in Greece die. For they are killed in the war against the Trojans.

IV.

1. οἱ ἄνδρες θώρακας καὶ ἀσπίδας ἔχουσιν, ἀλλ᾽ οὐκ ἀγαθοί εἰσιν.
2. τὸ δίκαιον εἶναι καὶ τὸ τὴν ἀλήθειαν λέγειν μέρη τῆς ἀρετῆς τῷ τῶν ἀνθρώπων γένει.
3. τόδε (τοῦτο) τὸ ἔτος ἀρχή ἐστι πολέμου μακροῦ καὶ χαλεποῦ.
4. τὸ τέλος τῆς δίκης μένομεν· ὁ γὰρ κλὼψ τοῦ τοὺς πολίτας μὴ εὖ (καλῶς) πράττειν αἴτιός ἐστι.
5. ἀπὸ ἐκείνων τῶν τειχῶν ἡ τοῦ Σωκράτους μήτηρ τὴν φωνὴν τὴν τοῦ ἐν τῇ ἀγορᾷ ῥήτορος ἀκούει.

6. τίς δαίμων τοὺς στρατιώτας βλάπτει; τίνι (τίσι) τῶν θεῶν οἱ στρατηγοὶ τὰ
   γέρα νῦν φέρουσιν;

7. παρὰ (ἐκ, πρὸς) τίνων λαμβανει ἐκεῖνα τὰ παιδία τὸ μέρος τῶν βιβλίων;

UNIT SIXTEEN

I.

1. you (pl.) were being asked *or* you (pl.) were asking for yourself — 2 pl. impf. m./p. ind. of αἰτέω

2. she *or* he *or* it was leading away — 3 s. impf. act. ind. of ἀπάγω

3. you (s.) hold off (*or* are distant) — 2 s. pres. act. ind. of ἀπέχω

4. they were praising *or* I was praising — 3 pl. impf. act. ind. of ἐπαινέω *or* 1 s. impf. act. ind. of ἐπαινέω

5. to desire — pres. act. inf. of ἐπιθυμέω

6. we were seeking — 1 pl. impf. act. ind. of ζητέω

7. they were leading *or* they believed — 3 pl. impf. m./p. ind. of ἡγέομαι

8. she *or* he *or* it was being prevented — 3 s. impf. m./p. ind. of κωλύω

9. she *or* he *or* it was *or* I was — 3 s. impf. act. ind. of εἰμί *or* 1 s. impf. act. ind. of εἰμί

10. to be led astray — pres m./p. inf of παράγω

11. she *or* he *or* it provided — 3 s. impf. act. ind. of παρέχω

12. we were turning — 1 pl. impf. act. ind. of τρέπω

13. they are leading *or* they believe — 3 pl. pres. m./p. ind. of ἡγέομαι

14. you (s.) were on your guard *or* you were being guarded — 2 s. impf. m./p. ind. of φυλάττω

15. you (pl.) were doing wrong — 2 pl. impf. act. ind. of ἀδικέω

16. I was perceiving — 1 s. impf. m./p. ind. of αἰσθάνομαι

17. you (s.) are becoming — 2 s. pres. m./p. ind. of γίγνομαι

18. it was necessary — 3 s. impf. act. ind. of δεῖ (*or* δέω)

19. they seemed *or* I seemed — 3 pl. impf. act. ind. of δοκέω *or* 1 s. impf. act. ind. of δοκέω

20. it was being inhabited *or* managed — 3 s. impf. m./p. ind. of οἰκέω

21. I was exhorting — 1 s. impf. m./p. ind. of παρακελεύομαι

22. they are learning by inquiry — 3 pl. pres. m./p. ind. of πυνθάνομαι

23. you (s.) were pouring a libation   2 s. impf. act. ind. of σπένδω

24. she *or* he was fleeing   3 s. impf. act. ind. of φεύγω

25. I was afraid   1 s. impf. m./p. ind. of φοβέω

26. it was being accomplished *or* she *or* he was accomplishing for herself *or* himself   3 s. impf. m./p. ind. of πράττω

27. they were   3 pl. impf. act. ind. of εἰμί

28. we were being arranged   1 pl. impf. m./p. ind. of τάττω

29. you (pl.) were being helped *or* you (pl.) are being helped *or* be helped (pl.)   2 pl. impf. m./p. ind. of ὠφελέω *or* 2 pl. pres. m./p. ind. of ὠφελέω *or* 2 pl. pres. m./p. impt. of ὠφελέω

30. it is being carried *or* she *or* he is winning   3 s. pres. m./p. ind. of φέρω

31. they were entrusting *or* I was entrusting   3 pl. impf. act. ind. of ἐπιτρέπω *or* 1 s. impf. act. ind. of ἐπιτρέπω

32. I am being made *or* I am making for myself   1 s. pres. m./p. ind. of ποιέω

33. she *or* he was seeking   3 s. impf. act. ind. of ζητέω

34. to be prevented   pres. m./p. inf. of κωλύω

35. they were being arrested   3 pl. impf. m./p. ind. of ἀπάγω

36. it was happening *or* she *or* he was becoming   3 s. impf. m./p. ind. of γίγνομαι

37. to be asked *or* to ask for oneself   pres. m./p. inf. of αἰτέω

38. we wanted   1 pl. impf. m./p. ind. of βούλομαι

39. they were ill *or* I was ill   3 pl. impf. act. ind. of νοσέω *or* 1 s. impf. act. ind. of νοσέω

40. you (s.) were inquiring   2 s. impf. m./p. ind. of πυνθάνομαι

41. you (s.) supposed   2 s. impf. m./p. ind. of οἴομαι

42. we were taking   1 pl. impf. act. ind. of λαμβάνω

II.

1. ἐφέρετο *or* ἤγετο
2. ἐφοβούμεθα
3. φιλεῖσθαι
4. ὠφέλουν
5. ἔπασχον
6. ἐμάχου
7. ἐλαύνειν
8. ἦτε *or* ἦστε
9. ἀπῆγε(ν)
10. ἀφικνοῦντο
11. ἡγεῖσθε
12. παρήγοντο

13. ζητοῦμεν	19. ἐλείπετε	25. φυλάττῃ
14. ἠσθάνετο	20. ᾤου	26. ἀπέχει
15. ἐπυνθανόμην	21. ἔμενον	27. ἐγράφετο
16. ἐδοκοῦμεν	22. ἐπεθύμουν	28. ἐβλάπτομεν
17. ποιεῖται	23. ἐκώλυον	29. ἀκούεται
18. ἔλεγε(ν)	24. παρέχεσθαι	30. ηὕρισκες

III.

1. In this place the noble and good men were unwilling to harm their fatherland and seize wealth, but they wanted not to be harmed by the bad men. But at that time it was possible for the bad men, who were always longing for office and wealth, to control this country. For they put the generals to death, and they lead the orators off to the shrine and guard them there. Then they were preventing the common people from deliberating concerning the affairs.

2. These terrible things the daughters of Demosthenes hear from the old man and immediately they kept asking the young men to lead them out of that country, in which were wild beasts and harmful birds [OR *harmful animals and birds*].

3. Then Pausanias encouraged the Athenians to send heralds concerning peace; and they [i.e., the Athenians] heeded him.

4. (Cf. Xen. *Anab.* 2.5.31–32.) And when they were at the doors of Tissaphernes, the generals go into the tent, while the soldiers were waiting at the doors. And after a short time [literally, *after no long time*] the former were being seized, and the latter were being cut down. Then the foreigners were riding across the plain and killing the Greeks.

5. Child *or* Son, do not praise bad men. For in what respect *or* toward what end do these fellows help their friends?

6. The sailors wanted to arrive at this country, but they were always turned toward another (land) by the winds.

7. The fortune of human beings is provided by the (tutelary) divinity [OR *by their destiny*], and now it is good, but hereafter *or* then again it is bad.

8. By these specious arguments those clever at speaking were misleading the others, but not Demosthenes, who was guarding the rights of the people.

9. While the Athenians were seeking a guide for the route, the allies were capturing wild animals alongside the river.

UNIT SEVENTEEN

I.

1. ἡγεμόσι τισί(ν)
2. θυγατρός τινος (or του)
3. Ἕλληνές τινες
4. σοφόν τινα στρατιώτην or σοφὸν
   στρατιώτην τινά or στρατιώτην
   τινὰ σοφόν or στρατιώτην σοφόν
   τινα
5. κράτος μικρόν τι or κράτος τι μικρόν
   or μικρόν τι κράτος or μικρὸν κράτος
   τι
6. ἀντὶ πληγῆς τινος (or του) or ἀντί
   τινος (or του) πληγῆς
7. διά τινα τῶν εὐχῶν or διὰ τῶν
   εὐχῶν τινα
8. πρὸς στενῇ τινι (or τῳ) ὁδῷ or πρὸς
   ὁδῷ τινι (or τῳ) στενῇ
9. τῶν ὁπλιτῶν τινας
10. παρὰ διδασκάλῳ τινί (or τῳ) or
    παρά τινι (or τῳ) διδασκάλῳ
11. σὺν θεαῖς τισι(ν) or σύν τισι θεαῖς
    or μετά τινων θεῶν or μετὰ θεῶν
    τινων
12. ἔν τινι (or τῳ) τῶν σκηνῶν or ἐν
    τῶν σκηνῶν τινι (or τῳ)

II.

1. The general of the Greeks remains (or remained) in that country for ten days
   and takes money from the foreigners who live by the sea. And the old men and
   the mothers were afraid for the children, but some good hoplites were preventing the sailors from doing any harm to them.
2. After this, the army marches (or marched) seven stades and arrives (or arrived)
   at a river, Chalos by name, and at a certain old bridge that a large number of
   strong men were guarding.
3. The teacher was making the accusation, the thief was the defendant, and the
   rich men were serving as jurors.
4. The previous resolution comes (or came) about in the aforementioned way, the
   later resolution in the following way: the multitude (or the common people)
   obeyed Demosthenes.
5. The old men were looking for the ancient writings, but for a long time they [i.e.,
   the writings] were being concealed by some children.
6. These men find the fellow in the marketplace and immediately were eager
   to arrest him or lead him away; but Isaeus and some others guard him and
   wanted to provide him to (or produce him at) the Assembly of the people.
7. The thieves were easily carrying the property from the camp, while the guards
   were not noticing it. For they were turning their eyes toward the enemies, who
   were seven stades away and were exhorting each other with powerful voices.

8. By the plans (*or* designs) of the divinity, lions have few children; for he wanted the other beasts to fare well and not always suffer bad things at the hands of the lions.

9. A man and not a man throws and does not strike a bird and not a bird with a stone and not a stone. [Compare the scholion on Plato, *Rep.* 479c: in the full form, a eunuch (man and not man) throws (one sense of βάλλω) a piece of pumice (stone and not stone) at a bat (bird and not bird) perched on a reed (wood and not wood) and fails to hit it (another sense of βάλλω).]

III.

1. *τίνα χρὴ ταύτην τὴν σοφίαν διαφέρειν; τὸν διδάσκαλον.*
2. *τότε ἐκεῖνα τὰ δεινὰ τοῦ ἡγεμόνος κατηγορεῖτε.*
3. *ἡγεῖτό τις τοῖς στρατιώταις ἀπὸ τοῦ τῶν πολεμίων στρατοπέδου στενὴν ὁδόν.*
4. *τοὺς πόδας κρύπτειν πως ἐβούλετο, ἀλλ᾽ ὁ δαίμων ἀεὶ ἐκώλυε(ν).*
5. *τὸν θῆρα ὕδωρ αἰτοῦσι· τοῖς γὰρ ἀνθρώποις ἐστὶν τρόπον τινὰ φίλιος.*
6. *πῶς καὶ ποῦ χρὴ τὴν ἀλήθειαν ζητεῖν;*

UNIT EIGHTEEN

For more information on future middle forms attested in classical Attic with passive meaning, see H. W. Smyth, *Greek Grammar*, rev. G. M. Messing (Cambridge, Mass. 1956) §§808–9; R. Kühner and B. Gerth, *Grammatik der griechischen Sprache. Zweiter Teil: Satzlehre* (Hanover 1898) I.114–17.

I.

1. to be called *or* about to be called
2. we shall learn
3. they will believe
4. they will fall
5. he will do wrong
6. you (pl.) will ask
7. about to throw
8. you (pl.) will pray
9. I shall be in need of *or* I shall ask for
10. you (s.) will excel
11. I shall leave
12. she *or* he will suppose
13. you (pl.) will die
14. she will beat herself [in mourning] *or* he will beat himself
15. it will be possible
16. she *or* he will exhort
17. I shall desire
18. you (s.) will hide yourself *or* you (s.) will conceal (for your own benefit)
19. about to have
20. we shall be distant *or* we shall hold off
21. you (s.) will kill
22. you (s.) will arrive

23. you (s.) will be
24. I shall flee
25. about to send
26. about to suffer (πάσχω) *or* about
    to obey (πείθω)

27. they will take
28. about to terrify
29. you (pl.) will say
30. she *or* he will praise

II.

1. οὐ καλῶς (or οὐκ εὖ)
   πράξομεν
2. σπείσονται
3. οὐ φοβήσεται
4. φυλάξεσθαι
5. ἔσεσθε
6. γυμνάσομαι

7. βαλοῦμεν
8. δεήσεσθε
9. ἐδόκει
10. νομιεῖν
11. κωλύσεις
12. ἡγήσονται
13. γράψεται

14. ἀδικησόμεθα
15. οἴσει
16. οὔποτε πεσοῦμαι
17. τρέψετε
18. πείσονται
19. ἐξέσται
20. οἰήσεται

III.

1. (Cf. Xen. *Anab.* 1.1.1.) Two children are born of (*or* to) Darius and Parysatis.
   (And) when Darius was about to die, he wanted his sons to be present. (And)
   he sends messengers to summon [literally, *who will summon*] Cyrus, and he
   [i.e., Cyrus] arrives in his father's presence. But later Cyrus will fight unjustly
   against his brother over the rule and he will neither fare well nor win victory,
   but will fall in the battle. And in the end his brother will rule instead of him.

2. Never will you learn even those small things, wretched man. For it will seem
   noble (*or* good) to the citizens not to be persuaded either by money or by blows
   to say these things.

3. (Cf. Lysias 12.4.) Cephalus, the father of Lysias, is persuaded by Pericles to
   come to the land of the Athenians, and he lives there for a long time and
   becomes wealthy.

4. Men, do good things for *or* benefit the common people in the same way in
   which your fathers once used to do it.

5. Virtue and pleasure are different. For the one will guide the soul toward what
   is noble, while the other will make someone unworthy of being praised.

6. We made these prayers to the gods for ten days. And *or* But what fortune will
   they now provide to the common army of the Greeks?

7. In the previous year we did not obey the foreign tyrant concerning the money,
   nor will we (*or* and we will not) pay tribute to him in the future.

IV.

1. οἱ Ἕλληνες τοὺς Ἀθηναίους ἡγεμόνας αἱρήσονται.
2. τοῦτο ὃ λέξειν μέλλω δεινόν ἐστιν, ἀλλὰ τὴν ἀλήθειαν οὐ κρύψω. [Middle κρύψομαι is also idiomatic in such a phrase.]
3. οὔποτε οὔτε ὁ ναύτης οὔτε ὁ δικαστής τινα ἐκείνων τῶν πλουσίων πολιτῶν βλάψει τι.
4. τὸ μηδὲ τοὺς παῖδας φοβεῖσθαι τὴν στρατιὰν ὠφελήσει.
5. ἐκεῖνα τὰ ἔτη δέκα τριήρεις εἴχομεν.

UNIT NINETEEN

I.

1. about to announce
2. to announce (aor.)
3. you (s.) led
4. to choose (aor.)
5. we perceived
6. take *or* seize (pl.)
7. you (s.) threw
8. you (s.) were throwing
9. you (pl.) bore
10. it *or* she *or* he seemed
11. exercise yourself (s.)
12. she *or* he led (*or* believed) *or* she *or* he came to believe
13. about to remain
14. to remain (pres.)
15. you (s.) exhorted
16. praise (s.)
17. you were fighting
18. I shall be distant *or* shall hold off
19. to provide (aor.)
20. it happened *or* it came about *or* she *or* he became
21. you (pl.) concealed
22. I carried across *or* they carried across *or* I proved superior (*or* I surpassed) *or* they proved superior (*or* they surpassed)
23. we took
24. I shall train [someone else]
25. you (s.) exercised
26. pray (pl.)
27. she *or* he came
28. to fight (aor.)
29. you (s.) inquired
30. inquire *or* learn by inquiry (s.)
31. say *or* speak (s.)
32. you (pl.) hoped *or* you (pl.) came to hope
33. to say (aor.)
34. we were
35. they put themselves on their guard *or* they guarded themselves against
36. we began *or* we ruled
37. I provided *or* they provided
38. we found
39. they made a truce
40. to seek (aor.)
41. she *or* he *or* it died
42. to learn (aor.)

II.

1. παρασχεῖν
2. ἐπέσομεν
3. ἐνεγκεῖν or ἐνέγκαι
4. ἐφύγομεν
5. εἶδες
6. παρήγαγον
7. παρῆγον
8. σχεῖν
9. ἀγγέλλουσι
10. ἐλπιεῖν
11. εἶπε(ν)
12. ἐγένεσθε
13. καλέσατε
14. ἀφικόμεθα
15. ἐβουλευσάμεθα
16. ἀκούσεται
17. κωλῦσαι
18. ἐδικάσαντο
19. ἀποκτενεῖν
20. ἑλέσθαι
21. ἀπέθανον
22. βάλλεις
23. ἐλπιῶ
24. εἴδομεν
25. ἄγγειλον
26. ἐπιτρέψαι
27. ἔδει or ἐχρῆν
28. ἐπυθόμεθα
29. πεσοῦμαι
30. ἐλπίσαι
31. ἐξῆν
32. ἐπαινέσαι
33. λύσασθαι
34. ἦλθες
35. διοίσω
36. ἐγράψαμεν
37. μάθετε or πύθεσθε
38. βούλευσαι

III.

1. The people by the sea used to fare well in other respects, but they suffered badly at the hands of some of the enemy who were always plundering the territory.

2. (Cf. Lysias 12.4–5.) Cephalus and his sons lived there for thirty years, and they never brought a suit or were defendants in a suit. For neither did they do harm to other men, nor did other men treat them unjustly. But when these villains seized the rule, they put Polemarchus to death because of his money, and Lysias with difficulty left the country. But in the end the allies of the democracy got the upper hand, and that man spoke in accusation of the impious men. For he was skilled at speaking.

3. The messenger came to the general and said: "I saw the enemy at the seven gates. Who will fight in each gate on behalf of the citizens? To which gods shall I order the mothers to pray? How will a victory come about? What must one do?" And he [i.e., the general] said: "There is no need to be afraid. For I have arranged the soldiers wisely (*or* skillfully) around the walls."

4. When the sailors announced the misfortunes of the army, both the mothers and the old men begged them to tell the name of each of the soldiers who fell in the battle.

5. Deliberate well, and choose this man as leader of the common people; for the earlier citizens often praised him.

6. The virtue of the jurymen became manifest at that time; for they did not entrust the money to the rich man but provided it to the children themselves.

7. We often summoned Socrates into the house, but he was seeking something wise and was not willing to come.

UNIT TWENTY

I.

1. we made a truce
2. they were being struck *or* they were striking themselves
3. they announced
4. you will excel *or* you will carry across
5. to take (aor.)
6. they will hope
7. they said *or* they were saying
8. to say (aor.)
9. about to learn
10. you (s.) recognize
11. she *or* he *or* it is called *or*

she *or* he *or* it will be called
12. we were beginning *or* we were ruling
13. you (s.) harmed
14. she *or* he suffered
15. you (pl.) say
16. you (s.) fell ill
17. I was praying
18. you (pl.) deliberated
19. she *or* he will arrive
20. you (s.) will be
21. I love

II.

1. ἄγομεν *or* ἡγούμεθα *or* ἄρχομεν
2. ἐβάλετε
3. δεήσει *or* χρῆσται
4. ἐπῄνεσα
5. ἡγήσεσθαι
6. λέγουσι(ν) *or* φασί(ν)
7. ᾠκοῦμεν
8. ᾖσθου
9. ἐβούλετο
10. ἐδόκουν
11. λέξομεν *or* ἐροῦμεν *or* φήσομεν
12. ἐκέλευον
13. ἔμαθε
14. παρασκευάζονται
15. ἀποθανῇ
16. γράψαι
17. ἦσθα
18. εὔχονται
19. κρύψεται
20. μενεῖς
21. ἐπείθομεν
22. εὑρεῖν

III.

1. (Cf. Lysias 1.5.) Euphiletus, who was on trial for murder, said the following to the jurors: "I shall narrate the affairs from the beginning and I shall not hide [anything]." For he believed that in this way he would persuade the citizens not to put him to death but to release him from [i.e., acquit him of] the charge.

2. How has some one of the gods not harmed this man's judgment, (this man) who kept saying impious things about the sun and the winds and the other celestial phenomena, and who kept doing a very great deal of harm to the shrines of the Greeks? [Rhetorical question equivalent to "How can it not be the case that some one of the gods has harmed . . ." or "Surely some one of the gods has harmed . . ."]

3. (Cf. Xen. *Anab.* 1.3.5–6.) "And no one will ever say, my fellow soldiers, that I led Greeks to the Persians and then I abandoned the Greeks and chose the friendship of the Persians. But since you are unwilling to obey me, I shall obey you." This is what Clearchus said. For he believed that his fellow soldiers were to him both fatherland and friends and allies. And the soldiers, both his own and the rest, praised these things [i.e., statements].

4. The old man said that the thieves were about to carry away the money but that the guard prevented (them).

5. Do you believe that the gods will help the just people in the war?

6. We hope that this slave will announce a victory.

7. I was leading *or* They were leading different soldiers to different parts of the walls. *or* I was leading *or* They were leading some soldiers to one part of the walls and other soldiers to other parts.

8. Take away *or* Arrest this unjust man; for he says he will not obey the laws nor help the common people with his money.

9. Isaeus was superior to the others orators in virtue; for he neither longed for the same things (as they did) nor had the same opinion about the toils that the *or* a good citizen must endure.

10. That man believed that cowardly men seldom fall in war.

11. After they came into the land of the Athenians, the allies themselves also fell ill.

IV.

1. οὐ χρὴ ταῦτα πείθεσθαι ἐκείνοις τοῖς ῥήτορσιν, ἀλλὰ (χρὴ) βουλεύεσθαι καλῶς καὶ δικαίως καὶ τὴν ἀλήθειαν ζητεῖν.

2. ἡγούμεθα (or ἐνομίζομεν or ᾠόμεθα) ἄλλους ἄλλα διαφέρειν.

3. τοῖς νεανίαις ἔδοξε τὰς θυγατέρας τὰς τοῦ διδασκάλου ἀγαγέσθαι· ἤλπιζον γὰρ ἑκάστην καὶ καλὴν καὶ πλουσίαν ἔσεσθαι.

4. τοὺς Ἕλληνας οἴεσθε ἡγεμόνας αἱρήσεσθαι τοὺς Ἀθηναίους;

5. τὸν ῥήτορα οὐκ ἐνόμιζον ταύτην τὴν σοφίαν δεῖν διαφέρειν.

6. αὕτη (ἡ γυνὴ) τοὺς στρατιώτας ἔφη τοὺς δικαστὰς εἰς τὸ πρὸς τοῖς τείχεσιν ἱερὸν ἀπαγαγεῖν.

7. τί οἱ παῖδες (τὰ) δεινὰ καὶ βλαβερὰ ζητεῖν βούλονται; or τί τὰ παιδία (τὰ) δεινὰ καὶ βλαβερὰ ζητεῖν βούλεται;

UNIT TWENTY-ONE

I.

1. These men were put to death by the Persians. And when the king had got these men out of the way, terrible things happened to the city after that; for which things this man is to blame, for he himself persuaded the king to come against Greece.

2. (Cf. Xen. *Hell.* 4.1.15–16.) And Agesilaus got a trireme ready and ordered Callias to take the girl away (in it), and he himself went off to the sacred city, in which dwelt the priest of the foreign goddess. This city was ten stades distant from the king's town,* and in it was a river full of small fish.
    * The article goes with ἄστεως, and βασιλέως has no article, as is usually the case with βασιλεύς when it refers to the king of Persia.

3. The rich man said that he would entrust the cattle and the swine to his son immediately but that it was not possible (to entrust to him) the mares.

4. Different people praise different habits.

5. He exhorted the cavalrymen to guard the other of the (two) walls while he himself and the infantry guarded this one.

6. (Cf. Lysias 12.44–45.) Thus you were plotted against not only by the enemy but also by these fellow citizens, and you were prevented from doing anything good. And they believed that you were eager to be rid of the troubles of the city and that you would not feel concern about the other matters. For they were about to dissolve the democracy.

7. What we ourselves do with insolence, these (actions) harm us at a later time.

8. That wise man wrote ten books about nature and another ten about the virtue of women and their characters.

9. The son of Callias said that men are prevented by law *or* custom from accomplishing the acts that they by nature are eager to accomplish; but do not choose this man as teacher.

10. Since our city alone was willing to suffer terrible things on behalf of the Greeks, we became leaders of the others and acquired our empire.

11. I am not a murderer. For neither did I kill anyone by hand, nor did I plot anything unjust.

12. (Cf. Xen. *Anab.* 2.5.41.) Since these men are friendly both to you and to us, send them to Cyrus. For they will ask him for the money that we need.

13. (Cf. Andocides, *Myst.* 149.) And now, I beg of you *or* I beseech you, become for me like a father [literally, *in place of a father*] and like brothers and like children.

II.

1. ἐκείνην μὲν τὴν ἡμέραν οἱ ἱππῆς τὸ στρατόπεδον ἐφύλαττον, τῇ δὲ ὑστέρᾳ (ἡμέρᾳ) πρὸς τοὺς πολεμίους ἤλασαν· ἡγοῦντο γὰρ ῥᾳδίως αὐτοὺς κρατήσειν.

2. ἡ ἔρις (or ἡ στάσις) καὶ ἡ ὕβρις τῇ πόλει τὸν αὐτὸν τρόπον βλαβεραί εἰσιν· ἑκατέρα τοῦ ἀγαθοὺς ἄνδρας ἀποθανεῖν αἰτία ἐστίν.

3. τοῦ βασιλέως ἐδεόμεθα ταῦτα (τὰ πράγματα) ταῖς γυναιξὶν αὐταῖς ἐπιτρέψαι.

4. οἱ μὲν γέροντες τὰς γυναῖκας τοῖς νόμοις δεῖν πείθεσθαι ἔφασαν, αἱ δὲ γρᾶες τοὺς ἄνδρας δεινῶν κακῶν τῇ πόλει γενέσθαι αἰτίους.

5. οἱ λέοντες φύσει ἰσχυροὶ καὶ δεινοί εἰσιν καὶ μόνοι τὰ ἄλλα θηρία (or τοὺς ἄλλους θῆρας) οὐ φοβοῦνται.

UNIT TWENTY-TWO

I.

1. τούτων or τῶνδε τῶν ἀσθενῶν βοῶν
2. πόλιν τινὰ τῆς στάσεως πλήρη
3. πρὸς τοὺς ἄφρονας κλῶπας
4. βραχὺν χρόνον
5. πᾶσαι αἱ γυναῖκες or πᾶσαι γυναῖκες
6. παρὰ τῷ χαρίεντι βασιλεῖ
7. τοῦ εὐδαίμονος ἱερέως
8. συμφορᾶς βαρείας
9. τὴν πᾶσαν ἰσχὺν τὴν τοῦδε τοῦ ἄστεως
10. κατὰ τὸν ἀληθῆ λόγον
11. μέτρῳ τινὶ ἀσφαλεῖ or διὰ μέτρου τινὸς ἀσφαλοῦς
12. οἱ ἐμοὶ δυστυχεῖς υἱοί or οἱ δυστυχεῖς υἱοί μου
13. εἰς ποταμὸν βαθὺν (καί) ὕδατος γλυκέος πλήρη
14. περὶ τῆς ὑμετέρας (or σῆς) ψευδοῦς νίκης or περὶ τὴν ὑμετέραν (or σὴν) ψευδῆ νίκην
15. δέκα σώφροσι γραυσί
16. νῆες μέλαιναι
17. ὁ βίος ἡμῶν ἡδύς. or ὁ ἡμέτερος βίος ἡδύς.
18. οἱ ἡμίσεις στρατιῶται ἀπέθανον. or οἱ ἡμίσεις τῶν στρατιωτῶν ἀπέθανον.
19. ἡ σὴ (or ὑμετέρα) θυγάτηρ οὐκ ἀφίκετο. or ἡ θυγάτηρ σου (or ὑμῶν) οὐκ ἀφίκετο.
20. ὑπὲρ ἡμῶν or πρὸ ἡμῶν
21. τὰς φύσεις ὑμῶν or τὰς ὑμετέρας φύσεις
22. χειρὶ ἰσχυρᾷ

II.

1. On each day the master used to lead his male slaves to the (agricultural) work, while he entrusted to his wife the female slaves and ordered her to guard the house and the property. For he believed that the natures of men and women were (*or* are) different.

2. How shall I tell you the true details, when what I must report is terrible?

3. When he supposed that your multitude (*or* you, the common people,) no longer wanted to listen to the speeches of the other speakers, then at last, both because of his jealousy toward those men and because he feared your power, he said that he himself mightily loved the common people.

4. Not only in war but also in a contest the weakness of old age and the strength of the young men prevent old men from fighting against them.

5. In this way we will inhabit our city safely, and we will become rich in regard to what concerns our livelihood, and we will always have the same opinion about public affairs.

III. (Cf. Xen. *Mem.* 2.1.21–33, a story ascribed to the sophist Prodicus)

Heracles was once deliberating about his life in a manner something like this: "What should I do? Shall I choose the road through (*or* of) virtue, or the other one?" Two women came up to him, one being self-controlled and nobly born, the other charming but bad. And they tried to persuade the man in turn. The latter said, "You must make *me* your friend, for I will lead you on the pleasant and easy path, and you will have all sweet things and avoid all hard things." And Heracles said, "Woman, what is your name?" She replied, "My friends call me Happy Prosperity, but the others call me Vice." The second woman said: "The path that I say you ought to choose is neither short nor safe nor easy. But it is not possible to become a truly noble and good man without toil. For the fine things are difficult, but all men and all gods will praise you." This woman's name was Virtue.

IV.

1. πάντας τοὺς ἡμετέρους ὁπλίτας ἀνάγκη γυμνάζεσθαι· τοῦτο γὰρ ἰσχυροὺς τὴν χεῖρα καὶ ἀγαθοὺς τὴν ψυχὴν αὐτοὺς ποιεῖ.

2. αἱ γρᾶες τὸν μὲν ἄνδρα ἔφασαν πλούσιον καὶ αἰσχρὸν καὶ χαλεπὸν εἶναι, τὴν δὲ γυναῖκα χαρίεσσαν καὶ ἡδεῖαν.

3. ὁ στρατηγὸς πάντα ταῦτα τὰ ἀγαθὰ τὴν πόλιν ἐποίησεν, ἀλλὰ διὰ τοὺς πονηροὺς ῥήτορας οἳ ψευδῆ αὐτοῦ κατηγόρησαν ὑφ᾽ ὑμῶν ἀπέθανεν.

UNIT TWENTY-THREE

I.

1. to display (aor.) — aor. act. inf. of ἐπιδείκνυμι
2. you (s.) are handing over — 2 s. pres. act. ind. of παραδίδωμι
3. they will release — 3 pl. fut. act. ind. of ἀφίημι
4. you (s.) were sending on — 2 s. impf. act. ind. of ἐφίημι
5. to go away (pres.) — pres. act. inf. of ἄπειμι (go away)
6. it was being set down — 3 s. impf. m./p. ind. of καθίστημι
7. to set free (pres.) — pres. act. inf. of ἀφίημι
8. she or he or it will go — 3 s. pres. act. ind. of εἶμι
9. you (pl.) are giving a share of — 2 pl. pres. act. ind. of μεταδίδωμι
10. she or he is causing to stand — 3 s. pres. act. ind. of ἵστημι
11. about to give — fut. act. inf. of δίδωμι
12. she or he was setting up — 3 s. impf. act. ind. of ἀνατίθημι
13. they are being yoked — 3 pl. pres. m./p. ind. of ζεύγνυμι
14. she or he was breaking — 3 s. impf. act. ind. of ῥήγνυμι
15. they were going out — 3 pl. impf. act. ind. of ἔξειμι (go out)
16. I am attacking — 1 s. pres. m./p. ind. of ἐπιτίθημι
17. they are betraying — 3 pl. pres. act. ind. of προδίδωμι
18. you (s.) were giving — 2 s. impf. act. ind. of δίδωμι
19. we shall go — 1 pl. pres. act. ind. of εἶμι
20. it was being shattered — 3 s. impf. m./p. ind. of ῥήγνυμι
21. you (s.) were being appointed — 2 s. impf. m./p. ind. of ἀποδείκνυμι
22. you (s.) are showing — 2 s. pres. act. ind. of δείκνυμι
23. you (pl.) will put down — 2 pl. fut. act. ind. of κατατίθημι
24. we are handing over — 1 pl. pres. act. ind. of παραδίδωμι
25. I aim at or I give orders — 1 s. pres. m./p. ind. of ἐφίημι
26. they will establish — 3 pl. fut. act. ind. of καθίστημι
27. she or he is giving a share of — 3 s. pres. act. ind. of μεταδίδωμι
28. you (s.) are hurling — 2 s. pres. act. ind. of ἵημι
29. you (s.) are in charge of — 2 s. pres. m./p. ind. of ἐφίστημι
30. to be betrayed (pres.) — pres. m./p. inf. of προδίδωμι
31. they were letting come to themselves — 3 pl. impf. m./p. ind. of προσίημι

32. to sell (pres.) *or* to be given back (pres.)   pres. m./p. inf. of *ἀποδίδωμι*

33. I am revolting from   1 s. pres. m./p. ind. of *ἀφίστημι*

34. you (s.) are placing   2 s. pres. act. ind. of *τίθημι*

35. I was being given   1 s. impf. m./p. ind. of *δίδωμι*

36. they are hastening *or* they are being let go   3 pl. pres. m./p. ind. of *ἵημι*

37. you (s.) are offering   2 s. pres. act. ind of *δίδωμι*

38. they are setting in charge of *or* they cause to stop   3 pl. pres. act. ind. of *ἐφίστημι*

39. to make an agreement (pres.) *or* to be put together (pres.)   pres. m./p. inf. of *συντίθημι*

40. you (pl.) will go out   2 pl. pres. act. ind. of *ἔξειμι* (go out)

41. I was yoking   1 s. impf. act. ind. of *ζεύγνυμι*

42. you (s.) were placing upon   2 s. impf. act. ind. of *ἐπιτίθημι*

II.

1. *ἴασι(ν)*
2. *ἀφίεμεν*
3. *κατατίθης*
4. *ῥηγνύναι*
5. *ἀνετίθετο*
6. *προδίδοτε*
7. *συνθήσεσθαι*
8. *ῥῆξαι*
9. *μετεδίδοσαν*
10. *ζεύγνυμεν*
11. *καθίστησι(ν)* or *ἀποδείκνυσι(ν)*
12. *ἀπιέναι*
13. *ἐζεύγνυτο*
14. *προσίεται*
15. *ἀφίσταμαι*
16. *ἐπιτίθεσθε*
17. *ἐπιδεικνύασι(ν)*
18. *ἐρρήγνυς*
19. *ἄπει*
20. *ἐφιέμεθα*
21. *ἵεμεν*
22. *τίθεται*
23. *ἀπεδιδόμην*
24. *ἱστᾶσι(ν)*

III.

1. Our allies are revolting from us, our enemies are attacking our walls, our generals are betraying the cities, but you citizens do not admit the messengers concerning peace.

2. Foolish people think that they will always be fortunate, while prudent people believe that the affairs (*or* fortunes) of humans are never secure.

3. After the victory of the enemy army in front of the town the slaves were leaving their masters' houses and were going away to the enemy.

4. Now it will be possible for the fellow to speak on behalf of peace, because the old men are no longer pelting him with stones. But earlier they believed that this man was about to betray the city.

5. The property that the Athenians used to dedicate to the goddess was sacred.

6. Each day those who are unfortunate yoke the oxen and prepare themselves to go to their works; for it is necessary for humans to have toils and find livelihood for themselves.

7. Peisistratus makes an agreement with the leaders of the other factions in the city and is established as tyrant *or* establishes himself as tyrant.

8. You were trying to give the ancient books to the priestesses, but they were unwilling to accept them.

9. Socrates said that the soul naturally aims for wisdom.

10. (Cf. Xen. *Hell.* 2.3.52–53.) Theramenes jumped up onto the altar and said: "Gentlemen, *I* believe that Critias ought not to be able to put me to death, but that the judgment (*or* trial) for both you and for me must be according to this law that these men wrote concerning those in the register [of citizens]. And *this* point is clear, that this altar will not help me at all, but I want to demonstrate this fact as well, that these men are not only unjust toward people but also impious toward gods."

UNIT TWENTY-FOUR

I.

1. they crossed
2. you (pl.) sold
3. to attack (aor.)
4. you (s.) stripped off [someone else's clothes *or* armor]
5. to give back (aor.)
6. she *or* he let go *or* sent on
7. to come to an agreement (aor.) *or* to happen (aor.)
8. you (pl.) set in charge of
9. I put down
10. you (s.) undressed [yourself]
11. I was established *or* I became
12. she *or* he distinguished
13. to cause to revolt (aor.)
14. we were captured
15. they will go out
16. to aim at (aor.) *or* to command (aor.)
17. to read aloud (aor.)
18. you (pl.) will go
19. to be captured
20. about to transgress
21. you (s.) gave back
22. she *or* he was setting down *or* appointing
23. they were coming together *or* I was coming to terms
24. they are being captured
25. you (s.) transgressed
26. they recognized
27. it sank
28. she *or* he placed upon
29. they admitted [to their presence]
30. you (pl.) gave a share of
31. they were
32. you (s.) dedicated
33. to show (pres.)

34. they will recognize
35. to put together (aor.)
36. you (pl.) were captured
37. we appointed
38. she *or* he became in charge of *or* stood upon *or* came to a stop
39. you (s.) attacked
40. she *or* he *or* it was being handed over
41. we were distinguishing
42. to make an agreement (aor.)

II.

1. νῆες ἑπτὰ κατέδυσαν.
2. δέκα τριήρεις κατεδύσαμεν.
3. ἐπέθεσθε
4. προδοῦναι
5. ἐγενόμεθα *or* κατέστημεν
6. ἡλίσκοντο
7. προσέσθαι
8. διαβήσεσθε
9. ἐκεῖνος ὁ νεανίας τοῦ σώφρων εἶναι ἐφεῖτο.
10. ἐπετίθεσο
11. ἀνέβησαν
12. ἀνέγνωτε
13. παρέδομεν
14. ἀπέστησας
15. πάντες ἑάλωσαν *or* ἥλωσαν.
16. παρέβη
17. ἡ τοῦ βασιλέως γυνὴ ἀπέδυ.
18. οὐκ ἔγνωμεν
19. συνέθεντο

III.

1. (Cf. Herodotus 5.95.) In that war other wondrous things happened in the battles, and Alcaeus the poet escaped (from the danger) himself but left behind his shield, and the Athenians captured it and dedicated it to the gods.

2. (Cf. Lysias 16.1.) These men want me to be caught (*or* found guilty) in this trial by every conceivable means, but you, do not be misled by their false statements but always seek to distinguish the truly just and the unjust.

3. (Cf. Xen. *Hell.* 2.3.43.) It is not these men—the ones who prevent enemies from being made numerous—who make your enemy strong and betray your friends, but rather those men, who unjustly take money away (from others) and put just men to death.

4. (Cf. in part Thuc. 2.36.1.) How is our city superior to the others? What need is there to say what everyone has heard? For the same people always inhabited the land, and our (fore)fathers handed down to us a city that was free because of excellence *or* bravery.

5. (Cf. Antiphon, *De Caede Herodis* 31.) The slave told the jurors about the unjust actions of Demosthenes, and he hoped he would win his freedom.

6. (Cf. Thuc. 1.71.9.) Neither did the Athenians themselves have *or* enjoy quiet *or* calm, nor because of them was it possible for the other Greeks to do so.

7. (Cf. Plato, *Theat.* 166e.) Because of the sickness even sweet things seem to be bitter to those who are weak *or* ill.

IV.

3. (Cf. Lysias 12.92–97.) I am about to step down [from the speaker's podium], gentlemen of the jury, but first I want to say a few words to each group, both to those from the town and to those from Piraeus. For I hope that you will hold (*or* regard) as examples the misfortunes that happened to you through these men and that you will cast your vote justly and wisely. You people from the town were ruled over harshly by these men, and because of these men you were waging a war against your brothers and sons and fellow citizens. You people from Piraeus were cast into exile from your fatherland and for no short time you were in need of all things, both money and friends, but in the end you came back home into Attica.

UNIT TWENTY-FIVE

I.

1. Great (*or* large) things are never secure.
2. You are the first who found for yourself (*or* obtained *or* earned) this honor.
3. Foolish is this man, who seems to himself to be powerful in all things (*or* to be able to do all things).
4. No one will be able to praise these men in a manner worthy of their noble actions.
5. (Cf. Plato, *Symp.* 175c.) And then, Aspasia said, Callias and some others left, but sleep overcame her.
6. When the general had summoned all the cavalrymen to himself, he distributed the money from the (Persian) king to each man.
7. (Cf. Thuc. 1.93.1.) In this manner the Athenians in a short time made their walls strong and tall, and so the Lacedaemonians were no longer able to (try to) attack them.
8. Peisistratus established himself as tyrant of the Athenians three times. For he was driven out twice, but finally through great toils he established himself with power over all things.
9. The foreigners were throwing many stones, so that it was necessary for each of the Greeks to be on his guard and to hold his shield up over his head.
10. Whereas the father was friendly and charming so that he was loved by all, each of his two sons says many bad things about the other so that they are praised by no one.
11. (Cf. Herodotus 5.93.) Socles said that he did not believe it was just for the Lacedaemonians to try to set up kingships in the cities, and all the others at

first kept themselves (in) quiet, but then every single one of them broke into speech and chose his [i.e., Socles'] opinion. And thus the allies commanded the Lacedaemonians to do nothing terrible concerning a Greek city.

12. (Cf. Lysias 19.18–20.) Aristophanes was always active in politics and was eager for honor. And so at that time together with Eunomus he went off to Sicily by ship, for he hoped to persuade Dionysius to become kinsman by marriage to Evagoras, hostile to the Lacedaemonians, and a friend and ally to your city. And there were many dangers related to the sea and the enemies, but nevertheless he tried to do these things, and finally he persuaded Dionysius not to send some triremes that at that time he had prepared for the Lacedaemonians.

II.

1. οἱ κλῶπες σοφοὶ ἔσονται ὥστε τοὺς ἄλλους τι τῶν πολλῶν ἀδίκων ἔργων κρύψαι;

2. οἱ σοφοὶ τοὺς ἀνθρώπους φασὶν ἀλλήλους ὠφελεῖν χρῆναι, ὥστε τοῦτο ποιοῦμεν.

3. οὕτως ἀγαθοὶ ἡμῖν αὐτοῖς δοκοῦμεν εἶναι ὥστε μηδένα ἡμῶν διαφέρειν.

4. τῷ φυγεῖν, ἄνδρες στρατιῶται, τὴν μάχην ἐποιήσατε πικρὰν μὲν ὑμῖν αὐτοῖς, ἡδεῖαν δὲ τοῖς πολεμίοις.

5. τέτταρας μὲν ἡμέρας ἐδύναντο οἱ ναῦται τοὺς ὁπλίτας ἀναβῆναι κωλῦσαι, τῇ δὲ πέμπτῃ (ἡμέρᾳ) ὀλίγοι ἐνόσησαν, ὥστε ἔδει ἑαυτοὺς παραδοῦναι.

UNIT TWENTY-SIX

I.

1. μαχούμενος, μαχουμένη, μαχούμενον

2. βαλών, βαλοῦσα, βαλόν

3. βουλόμενος, βουλομένη, βουλόμενον

4. παρατιθείς, παρατιθεῖσα, παρατιθέν

5. ἐπιδειξάμενος, ἐπιδειξαμένη, ἐπιδειξάμενον

6. νοσήσων, νοσήσουσα, νοσῆσον

7. (weak, 1st) ἀποδύσας, ἀποδύσασα, ἀποδῦσαν, (strong, 2nd) ἀποδύς, ἀποδῦσα, ἀποδύν

8. νομιῶν, νομιοῦσα, νομιοῦν

9. ἐφιέμενος, ἐφιεμένη, ἐφιέμενον

10. ἐξιών, ἐξιοῦσα, ἐξιόν

11. παραβησόμενος, παραβησομένη, παραβησόμενον

12. ἐπιθέμενος, ἐπιθεμένη, ἐπιθέμενον

II.

1. ἁρπασόμενος
2. τεμούσης
3. τρεφομένῳ
4. διαδώσοντα
5. γενόμεναι
6. ῥηγνύντων
7. πεισομένοις
8. κοψάσας
9. ἐπαινούμενον
10. καλοῦντος
11. μαχεσαμένη
12. δοκοῦν
13. ἀξόμενοι
14. ἀρξασῶν
15. γραφομένοις
16. πυνθανομένῳ
17. ἡγησόμενος
18. ἀποθανούσης
19. ἀποσχόντας
20. βλάψοντα
21. διαβάντας
22. οἰκούντων
23. ἀφησομένοις
24. ἰδούσας
25. γιγνόμενον
26. ἀποκτενοῦντος
27. καταστησαμένη
28. νομίζον
29. ἐσόμενοι
30. θεισῶν
31. ποιουμένοις
32. παρακελευσάμεναι

III.

1. nom. *or* voc. s. f. fut. mid. part. of εἰμί
2. dat. pl. f. fut. mid. part. of φεύγω
3. dat. s. m. *or* n. pres. act. part. of ἔξειμι
4. gen. s. m. *or* n. aor. mid. part. of σπένδω
5. dat. pl. m. *or* n. pres. act. part. of τάττω
6. acc. s. m. aor. act. part. of ἀφίημι
   or nom. *or* acc. *or* voc. pl. n. aor. act. part. of ἀφίημι
7. gen. pl. m. *or* n. pres. act. part. of ποιέω
8. nom. *or* voc. s. f. (strong, 2nd) aor. act. part. of φέρω
9. nom. *or* acc. *or* voc. pl. n. pres. m./p. part. of τίθημι
10. dat. pl. m. *or* n. (strong, 2nd) aor. act. part. of δύω
11. nom. *or* acc. *or* voc. s. n. fut. act. part. of πείθω
12. dat. pl. m. *or* n. fut. act. part. of βάλλω
    or dat. pl. m. *or* n. aor. act. part. of βάλλω
13. dat. s. f. pres. m./p. part. of ὑπισχνέομαι
14. acc. s. m. aor. act. part. of ἐσθίω
    or nom. *or* acc. *or* voc. pl. n. aor. act. part. of ἐσθίω
15. gen. pl. f. fut. act. part. of καίω
16. dat. s. m. *or* n. pres. act. part. of ἐφίστημι
17. acc. pl. m. fut. act. part. of ἐρέω
18. acc. s. m. pres. act. part. of εἰμί
    or nom. *or* acc. *or* voc. pl. n. pres. act. part. of εἰμί
19. dat. s. m. *or* n. aor. act. part. of παράγω
20. gen. s. m. *or* n. aor. act. part. of ἔχω
21. acc. s. m. aor. act. part. of ὠφελέω

or nom. *or* acc. *or* voc. pl. n. aor. act. part. of ὠφελέω

22. gen. pl. f. aor. act. part. of δίδωμι
23. acc. pl. m. (strong, 2nd) aor. act. part. of ἵστημι
24. acc. s. f. fut. act. part. of λείπω
25. nom. *or* voc. pl. f. (weak, 1st) aor. act. part. of ἵστημι
26. nom. *or* voc. pl. m. aor. act. part. of λαμβάνω
27. gen. s. m. *or* n. aor. mid. part. of ἀφικνέομαι
28. nom. *or* voc. s. m. aor. act. part. of φιλέω
29. nom. *or* voc. pl. f. aor. mid. part. of ἀποδίδωμι
30. acc. pl. m. aor. mid. part. of πυνθάνομαι

IV. (Cf. Herodotus 2.20–24.)

But certain of the Greeks, who wanted to show themselves to be notable in respect to wisdom, have spoken three ways of explaining concerning this water; two of which it is not worthwhile to speak of except in brief terms. Of these, the one says that the Etesian [i.e., annual] winds are responsible for the fact that the river becomes full (for [they say] the winds prevent the Nile from flowing out into the sea). But often the Etesian winds have not blown, but the Nile does the same thing. The second (explanation) is less scientific, the one that says that it flows from the Ocean, and that the Ocean flows around the entire earth. The third of the explanations is by far the most reasonable but is false. For not even this one makes sense [literally, *says anything*]; for it says that the Nile flows from melting snow.

But since I must display my own opinion concerning this, I will tell why (*or* on account of what) the Nile seems to me to flood during the summer. During the stormy season the sun is driven from its former (*or* old) path by the winter storms and it goes toward the inland parts of Africa. And the Nile alone is caused to evaporate by the sun in such a way that during this time it flows with little water, but during the summer it is evaporated equally with all the other rivers, and it flows with more water.

UNIT TWENTY-SEVEN

I.

1. κελεύσαντος τοῦ στρατηγοῦ πάντες παρὰ τὸν ποταμὸν ἤλαυνον φυλαττόμενοι.
2. οἱ τὸν ἐμὸν πατέρα ἀποκτείναντες δίκην δώσουσιν.
3. τὸ ἄστυ λιποῦσα εἰς τὴν θάλατταν κατέβη.
4. ὁ μαθεῖν μὴ ἐθέλων τὴν ψυχὴν νοσεῖ.
5. καίπερ πάντα ταῦτα ὑποσχόμενος ὅμως οὐδὲν ἔπραξεν.

6. στρεφόμενον (or τρεπόμενον or στρεψάμενον or τρεψάμενον) τὸ στράτευμα ἐπέστη.

7. ὕπνος βαθὺς τοὺς πολὺ πιόντας εἶχεν.

8. διωκόντων ἡμῶν τοὺς τὸν ποταμὸν διαβάντας οἱ Ἀθηναῖοι τὰς σκηνὰς καύσαντες τοὺς ἵππους ἥρπασαν.

9. τῷ βαρβάρῳ πειθόμεθα, καίπερ πολλὰ καὶ δεινὰ ἀγγέλλοντι.

10. ὡς οὐ πλούσιοι ὄντες τὰς τριήρεις παρασκευάζειν οὐ δυνήσονται.

II.

1. At the urging of the leaders (or archons), the citizens made peace with those who were in exile.

2. Although many cavalrymen were attacking, nevertheless we took up for burial those who had died.

3. Demosthenes promised he would do these things, speaking falsely.

4. Although it is necessary (or It being necessary) to care for one's parent (or the one who cared [for you]) in old age, the common mass of people are unwilling (to do so).

5. The fools among mankind let go of what is at hand and pursue what is absent.

6. Who will be able to win victory in the contest if he is not tall and strong?

7. (Cf. Xen. *Anab.* 1.1.3.) The king arrests Cyrus with the intention of putting him to death.

8. (Cf. Thuc. 2.40.2.) Each of us deliberates well about the affairs of the city; for we alone believe that any man who does not partake of these affairs is not a quiet but a bad citizen.

9. (Cf. Plato, *Menex.* 236c.) Do not beafraid, Socrates, but tell me the speech of Aspasia, and I will have *or* feel great gratitude toward you.

10. (Cf. Plato, *Menex.* 236d.) Do you command me to strip off my (outer) clothes and dance? I will do this since we are alone here.

11. (Cf. Lysias 28.13.) But I, gentlemen of Athens, do not have the same judgment about each of the two groups. These men, who longing for freedom and justice and wanting the laws to be valid and hating those who do wrong partook of your dangers, I believe are not bad citizens. But those men, who having returned home from exile under democracy are doing wrong to you, the common people, and are making their private households great using [literally, *out of*] your property, one must very vehemently accuse, just as one does the Thirty.

III. (*Anthologia Palatina* 7.348.) Having drunk a lot and eaten a lot and said a lot of bad things about (or having often insulted) my fellow men, here I lie, Timocreon of Rhodes.

UNIT TWENTY-EIGHT

I.

1. You will not err if you say this. *or* You will not be wrong in saying this.
2. The young man feels bad, for he never endures being second.
3. He happened to be taking exercise on that day.
4. You (pl.) did badly in allowing these women to be treated unjustly by the other women.
5. Who will get up to the acropolis before the foreigners? *or* Who will beat the foreigners in going up to the acropolis?
6. I will easily prove that he concealed this money.
7. Do you not know that death will stop both those who are faring well and those who are not?
8. (Cf. Isocr. *Panath.* 115.) Nobody ought to be angry at those who preferred our city instead of the other (of two). For these people have not been mistaken in their hopes (*or* have not failed to attain their hopes *or* to find their hopes fulfilled), nor were they at all unaware either of the good features or of the bad features that each of the two powers has.
9. (Cf. Isaeus, *De Hagnia* 36.) There is no need to speak about these matters (*or* these men) in lengthy fashion. For I suppose that you all know, gentlemen, that Callias spoke many things in (*or* by means of) perjury.
10. (Cf. Thuc. 7.38.3 and Xen. *Hell.* 7.1.49.) The Athenians continued getting these things ready for the entire day and stopped a little before the setting sun (*or* before sunset).

II. (Cf. Lysias 2.7–15)

When Adrastus and Polynices attacked Thebes and did not fare well in the battle, and the Thebans were preventing anyone from burying the dead bodies, the Athenians, since they judged (*or* believed) that the former had paid a sufficient penalty in dying, while the latter were committing an offense against the gods, first, having sent messengers, they asked them [i.e., the Thebans] to grant (the opportunity of) picking up the dead. When they were not able to obtain this (favor), they [i.e., the Athenians] went on campaign against them [i.e., the Thebans], even though there was previously no disagreement with the Thebans, because they [i.e., the Athenians] believed that those who had died ought to receive the customary rites. And because they [i.e., the Athenians] had justice as their ally, they were victorious in battle and displayed their excellence to all men.

At a later time, after Heracles had died, his children, in flight from Eurystheus, kept being driven out by all the Greeks, who, although ashamed at their deeds, were afraid of Eurystheus's power. And when the children came to this city, and Eurystheus was demanding their surrender to him, the Athenians did not consent to hand them over. And when the Argives came on campaign against them, they [i.e., the Athenians] did not change their minds when they got close to the terrible events, but they kept the same decision, and they were victorious in battle a second time.

UNIT TWENTY-NINE

I.

1. ἐκαύθησαν
2. ἀνατεθησομένοις
3. ὀργισθήσῃ
4. ἀνάγνωτε
5. ἐπράχθητε
6. ῥαγεῖσαν
7. ἐκρίθην
8. ἐλείφθημεν
9. τμηθῆναι
10. ἐφάνη or ἐφάνθη
11. ἐπαινεθήσεσθαι
12. βληθέν
13. σχεῖν
14. ἐπίθεσθε
15. ἀπόδος
16. ἀπόδυθι
17. αἱρεθήσονται
18. πρόσεσθε
19. ἐδιώχθησαν
20. ἡσθείς
21. μετάσχες
22. ἄπιτε
23. ἤχθημεν

II.

1. aor. pass. inf. of λαμβάνω
2. 3 s. fut. pass. ind. of ποιέω
3. 2 pl. fut. pass. ind. of βάλλω
4. 1 s. fut. pass. ind. of κωλύω
5. 2 pl. aor. act. ind. of διαγιγνώσκω
6. 2 s. aor. pass. ind. of νομίζω
7. 3 pl. aor. pass. ind. of τάττω
8. aor. mid. impt. of φυλάττω
9. aor. pass. inf. of αἰτέω
10. 2 pl. aor. act. impt. of παραδίδωμι
11. acc. s. m. aor. pass. part. of πράττω or nom. or acc. or voc. pl. n. aor. pass. part. of πράττω
12. 2 s. pres. act. impt. of ἀποδείκνυμι
13. 2 s. aor. pass. impt. of ἐπιτίθημι
14. nom. s. m. aor. pass. part. of ὠφελέω
15. dat. s. f. aor. pass. part. of κρατέω
16. 2 s. aor. pass. ind. of πείθω
17. nom. or acc. or voc. s. n. aor. pass. part. of κρύπτω
18. 2 s. aor. act. impt. of διαδίδωμι
19. acc. s. m. fut. pass. part. of ἁρπάζω or nom. or acc. or voc. s. n. fut. pass. part. of ἁρπάζω
20. 3 pl. aor. pass. ind. of ἐλαύνω
21. 1 pl. aor. pass. ind. of φοβέω or φοβέομαι
22. 3 s. aor. pass. ind. of ἐρέω
23. fut. pass. inf. of ἥδομαι
24. 3 s. aor. pass. ind. of περιοράω
25. 3 pl. fut. pass. ind. of εὑρίσκω
26. 1 s. aor. pass. ind. of ζητέω
27. gen. s. m. or n. aor. pass. part. of φαίνω
28. 2 s. fut. pass. ind. of φαίνω
29. 3 s. fut. pass. ind. of ἀγγέλλω
30. 3 s. aor. pass. ind. of ἀνατίθημι

31. 3 s. impf. act. ind. of ἀνατίθημι
32. 2 pl. aor. pass. ind. of ἀπάγω
33. 2 s. pres. act. impt. of ἐπίσταμαι
34. 2 pl. aor. act. ind. of ἀποδύω
    (intrans. 2nd *or* strong aorist)
35. aor. pass. inf. of γιγνώσκω
36. nom. *or* voc. pl. f. aor. pass. part. of
    δείκνυμι

37. 3 s. aor. pass. ind .of τρέφω
38. acc. s. m. aor. pass. part. of δύναμαι
    or nom. *or* acc. *or* voc. pl. n. aor.
    pass. part. of δύναμαι
39. 2 pl. aor. pass. ind. of ὀργίζομαι
40. 2 pl. aor. pass. impt. of ὀργίζομαι
41. 2 s. aor. pass. ind. of βάλλω
42. 2 pl. fut. pass. ind. of ποιέω

III.

1. Callias, sell the mares and dedicate many gifts to the gods.
2. Since, therefore, the allies have been prevented from coming, attack the Persians alone.
3. Know *this* fact (*or* at least this fact) clearly: in this peace all the Greeks will be wronged by that man.
4. (Cf. Isaeus 1.40.) Will you consider it to be just that another set of men share in the property that our father handed down to us? In that case, neither will you do just things, nor will you protect the laws, nor will you benefit yourselves.
5. (Dem. 5.24.) So then, must we do what is bidden because of fear of these things? Are *you too* recommending this course? —I am far from doing so.
6. (Cf. Isocrates 19.2.) And I am almost grateful (*or* I am close to feeling gratitude) to these men, who have put me into this legal contest.

IV.

At this point, ambassadors come from Sinope, fearing both concerning the city of the Cotyoritans (for it belonged to them, and the Cotyoritans paid tribute to them,) and concerning the (Cotyoritans') land (for they were hearing that it was being plundered). And having come into the camp they spoke (Hecatonymus, who was considered a skilled speaker, was their spokesman): "Gentlemen of the army, the city of the Sinopeans sent us both to praise you, because being Greeks you are defeating non-Greeks, and second, also to rejoice with you, because you are present here after coming safely through difficulties that were (as we have heard) many and terrible. And we think it proper that, since we are ourselves also Greeks, we receive from you, who are Greeks, some good treatment and suffer nothing bad. For neither have we on our part ever yet taken the initiative in doing harm to you. These people of Cotyora are our colonists, and we turned this territory over to them after taking it away from foreigners."

UNIT THIRTY

I.

1. 1 pl. impf. act. ind. of τελευτάω — we were accomplishing

2. 3 pl. impf. m./p. ind. of ζηλόω — they were being emulated

3. 3 pl. pres. m./p. ind. of τιμάω — they are being honored

4. 1 pl. impf. act. ind. of ὁράω — we were seeing

5. 3 pl. pres. act. ind. of διασκεδάννυμι — they are scattering

6. dat. pl. f. pres. act. part. of τιμάω — [to or for women] honoring

7. fut. act. inf. of μετέχω — about to have a share

8. 2 s. aor. act. ind. of ἀναμιμνῄσκω — you (s.) reminded

9. nom. or voc. s. m. aor. act. part. of ἀναμιμνῄσκω — (nom.) [man] having reminded or (voc.) [man] having reminded

10. 3 s. impf. act. ind. of νικάω — she or he was victorious

11. pres. m./p. inf. of ὁράω — to be seen (pres.)

12. 3. s. pres. act. ind. of ἐμπίμπλημι — she or he is filling

13. nom. or voc. s. m. fut. act. part. of διασκεδάννυμι — (nom.) [man] about to scatter or (voc.) [man] about to scatter or

    nom. or acc. or voc. s. n. fut. act. part. of διασκεδάννυμι — (nom.) [thing] about to scatter or (acc.) [thing] about to scatter or (voc.) [thing] about to scatter

14. 2 s. fut. act. ind. of ἐλαύνω — you (s.) will drive

15. 2 s. impf. act. ind. of ἐμπίμπλημι — you (s.) were filling

16. 1 pl. perf. act. ind. of οἶδα — we know

17. 3 s. fut. act. ind. of φαίνω — she or he or it will reveal

18. 2 s. pres. act. impt. of τιμάω — be victorious or win (s.)

19. pres. m./p. inf. of ζηλόω — to be emulated

20. dat. s. m. or n. pres. act. part. of ἀπορέω — [to or for a man] being at a loss [to or for a thing] being at a loss

21. nom. or acc. or voc. s. n. pres. m./p. part. of τελευτάω — (nom.) [thing] being accomplished or (acc.) [thing] being accomplished or (voc.) [thing] being accomplished or

    or acc. s. m. pres. m./p. part. of τελευτάω — (acc.) [man] being accomplished [masc. use unlikely]

22. 3 pl. impf. act. ind. of τιμάω — they were honoring
    or 1 s. impf. act. ind. of τιμάω — I was honoring

23. 2 s. impf. m./p. ind. of δηλόω — you (s.) were being revealed

24. 2 s. fut. mid. ind. of ἁρπάζω — you (s.) will seize

25. pres. m./p. inf. of ἐπίσταμαι — to know

26. 3 s. pres. act. ind. of δηλόω — she *or* he *or* it is revealing
    or 2 s. pres. m./p. ind. of δηλόω — you (s.) are being revealed

27. pres. act. inf. of τιμάω — to honor

28. 3 s. impf. act. ind. of ἀπορέω — she *or* he was at a loss

29. nom. *or* voc. pl. m. pres. m./p. part. of ζηλόω — (nom.) [men] being emulated *or* (voc.) [men] being emulated

30. 2 pl. pres. act. ind. of νικάω — you (pl.) win *or*
    or 2 pl. pres. act. impt. of νικάω — win *or* be victorious (pl.)

31. 1 s. pres. act. ind. of ὁράω — I see
    or 2 s. pres. m./p. impt. of ὁράω — be seen (s.)

32. 1 pl. impf. act. ind. of ἐμπίμπλημι — we were filling

33. 2 pl. pres. act. ind. of δηλόω — you (pl.) reveal
    or 2 pl. pres. act. impt. of δηλόω — reveal (pl.)

34. fut. act. inf. of τελευτάω — about to bring to an end

35. aor. act. inf. of φαίνω — to reveal (aor.)

36. 3 pl. fut. mid. ind. of οἶδα — they will know

37. 3 pl. fut. mid. ind. of εἰμί — they will be

38. dat. pl. f. fut. mid. part. of ὀργίζομαι — [to *or* for women] about to be angry

39. 3 s. aor. mid. ind. of παύω — she stopped herself *or* he stopped himself *or* it stopped itself

II.

1. ζηλοῦν and ζηλῶσαι
2. τελευτᾶν and τελευτῆσαι
3. νικῶσι(ν)
4. τὰ δηλούμενα or τὰ φαινόμενα
5. ἐνεπίμπλασαν
6. ζηλούμεθα
7. ἑώρας
8. τιμωμένης
9. διασκεδαννύναι and διασκεδάσαι
10. μεθέξοντας or μετασχήσοντας
11. ἀνεμνήσατε or ὑπεμνήσατε

12. ἐζήλουν
13. νικᾶσθαι or κρατεῖσθαι
14. ἑωρᾶτε
15. τιμώμεθα
16. ἑλῶμεν
17. μετέδωκε(ν)
18. μετεῖχον or μετέσχον
19. πείσεσθαι
20. πίνειν and πιεῖν
21. μνήσθητι
22. διασκεδάννυτε and διασκεδάσατε

III.

1. And three days later they again made their own virtue manifest by helping those who were lacking food.
2. It is obvious, fellow soldiers, that you are mindful neither of what happened then nor of what is now about to occur.
3. This villain was so clever at speaking that he appeared to be worthy of office.
4. At first the old man remained inactive (*or* kept quiet) when he saw these things being done by those who were plotting against the archons, but finally he revealed everything to the citizens in order to put a stop to the strife.
5. Since the Thebans were not coming out to battle, the Athenians continued building a wall of large stones, four stades distant from the walls of the town.
6. The king's soldiers are equal to the Greeks in number but not in valor.
7. Pentheus did not easily endure hearing that all the women were honoring the god who had come from Lydia.
8. When the father (had) died, the four sons were scattered, one to one city and another to another.
9. Take the grain and give a share of it to the women and children.
10. Aspasia was annoyed at not being honored by the priestesses.
11. The enemy cavalry have captured the bridge ahead of us. How, then, will it be possible to cross a river eleven cubits in depth?
12. (Cf. Lysias 7.1.) While formerly I used to believe that it was permitted to anyone who wanted, if he minded his business, to have neither court cases nor troubles, now everything comes about contrary to expectation, and I am being placed in (*or* am involved in) a terrible struggle (in court).
13. (Cf. Lysias 33.7.) I do not know what idea in the world the Lacedaemonians have when they permit Greece to be burned, since they are not unjustly leaders of the Greeks both because of their inborn virtue and because of their expertise in connection with war. [Literally, . . . *making use of what idea in the world the Lacedaemonians are permitting* . . .]

UNIT THIRTY-ONE

I.

1. ἀμείνονι γνώμῃ *or* μετὰ ἀμείνονος γνώμης
2. τὸν κάκιστον τρόπον *or* κάκιστα
3. ῥᾷον
4. τοῖς ἀκροτάτοις
5. ἐκ τοῦ ἀληθεστέρου λόγου
6. ταῖς ἀξιωτάταις (γυναιξίν)
7. τὴν ἀσφαλεστέραν ὁδόν

8. τὸν ἀδικώτατον τῶν τοῦ Κύρου στρατιωτῶν

9. τοῦ σοφωτάτου διδασκάλου

10. πλουσιωτέρου τινός or πλουσιωτέρου τινὸς ἀνδρός

11. φανερώτατα or δηλότατα or σαφέστατα

12. πλείω χρήματα or πλείονα χρήματα or πλέονα χρήματα

13. τῇ μεγίστῃ πόλει

14. ὡς χρηστότατον

15. τὸ ἥδιστον πάντων or τὸ γλυκύτατον πάντων

16. αἴσχιον, αἴσχιστα

II.

1. When the allies there had revolted, Peisistratus immediately marched on campaign against them with eighty hoplites.

2. (Cf. Thuc. 3.37.3.) A city that uses worse laws that the citizens obey is better than one that uses laws in fine condition *or* excellent laws that they don't obey.

3. (Cf. Antiphon, *Tetr.* 3.2.3.) This man said it is just that those who begin injustice suffer not the same things but greater and more numerous things.

4. (Cf. Antiphon, *Tetr.* 1.2.8.) I am most harshly wronged, but nevertheless I will continue refuting my enemies, for there is nothing more bitter than necessity.

5. (Cf. Isocr. 14.41.) In this way you will see within a few years all the cities being slaves to Lacedaemonians.

6. When civil strife had taken hold and many had died, the multitude trusted the oligarchic party no more easily than the oligarchs trusted the common people.

7. (Cf. Xen. *Apol.* 28.) But, Socrates, at *this* I am very sorely vexed: for I see you being put to death unjustly. —And you, my dearest friend, were you preferring to see me being put to death justly rather than unjustly?

III.

1. οὐκ ἀγνοοῦμεν τοὺς νεανίας τῶν γερόντων θάττους (or θάττονας) ὄντας. or οὐκ ἀγνοοῦμεν τοὺς νεανίας θάττους (or θάττονας) ἢ τοὺς γέροντας ὄντας.

2. πολλοῖς μὲν τῶν ῥητόρων ὀργιζόμενοι ἀγγέλλεσθε, μάλιστα δὲ (πάντων) τῷ Δημοσθένει. or πολλοῖς μὲν τῶν ῥητόρων ὀργιζόμενος (or ὀργιζομένη) ἀγγέλλῃ, μάλιστα δὲ (πάντων) τῷ Δημοσθένει.

3. τοὺς κλῶπας ἔλαθε ἡ ναῦς ἣν ἥρπασαν (or ἡ ἁρπασθεῖσα ναῦς) ὕδατος ἐμπιμπλαμένη. or οἱ κλῶπες οὐκ ᾔσθοντο τὴν ναῦν ἣν ἥρπασαν (or τὴν ἁρπασθεῖσαν ναῦν) ὕδατος ἐμπιμπλαμένην.

4. βουλευσαμένοις τοῖς Ἕλλησιν ἄμεινον ἔδοξε τὸ ἰσχυρότατον (μέρος) τῆς στρατιᾶς πρὸς τὴν θάλατταν πέμψαι ὥστε τὸ ἑαυτῶν πλῆθος τοὺς βαρβάρους ὡς πλεῖστον χρόνον κρύπτειν.

IV.

Once when the Assembly conceived a desire to put to death all those associated with Thrasyllus and Erasinides by a single vote contrary to the laws, Socrates, being a member of the Council and at that time getting his turn as (*or* having become) the presiding officer in the Assembly, refused to put the measure to the vote, even though the Assembly was becoming angry with him and many powerful men were threatening him. But he considered it of greater importance to abide by his oath than to oblige the Assembly contrary to justice and to guard himself against those threatening him. For indeed he believed that the gods have concern for human beings, not in the (same) way that most people believe. For *they* believe that the gods know some things and do not know others, but Socrates believed that the gods know everything, both what is being said and done and what is being planned in silence, and that the gods are present everywhere and give signs to men concerning all human affairs.

UNIT THIRTY-TWO

I.

1. σιγήσῃ	9. ἀφιστῇ	17. ἀπαγάγῃς
2. ἡττᾶσθε	10. ἐπιθυμήσωμεν	18. νοσῇ
3. δουλεύσῃς	11. κωλύωμαι	19. κρυφθῶ
4. ἀπορῇ	12. στρατευώμεθα	20. ἀναβῇ
5. ἐλέγχωνται	13. εἰδῶμεν	21. δύνησθε
6. μνησθῶσι	14. ἴῃς	22. ποιήσωσι(ν)
7. ἡττηθῇ	15. ἀφίκωνται	23. ἐθέλωμεν
8. ἐπιθῶμαι	16. καλέσωμαι	24. σπενδώμεθα

II.

1. 3 pl. aor. act. subj. of παρέχω
2. 3 s. pres. m./p. subj. of ἀναγιγνώσκω
3. 2 s. pres. act. subj. of ἄπειμι (be away)
4. 3 pl. aor. mid. subj. of αἱρέω
5. 2 s. aor. act. subj. of ἀφίημι
6. 2 s. perf. act. subj. of οἶδα
7. 2 pl. aor. act. subj. of βασιλεύω
8. 1 pl. pres. act. subj. of δείκνυμι
9. 3 s. aor. act. subj. of δηλόω
   or 2 s. aor. mid. subj. of δηλόω
   or 2 s. fut. mid. ind. of δηλόω
10. 3 pl. pres. act. subj. of διαμένω
11. 3 s. pres. act. subj. of διώκω
    or 2 s. pres. m./p. ind. *or* subj. of διώκω
12. 2 pl. aor. pass. subj. of ἄρχω
13. 3 pl. pres. m./p. subj. of δύναμαι
14. 2 pl. aor. mid. subj. of ἐξαιτέω

15. 2 pl. aor. act. subj. of παραβαίνω

16. 2 s. pres. m./p. ind. *or* subj. of κρύπτω
    or 3 s. pres. act. subj. of κρύπτω

17. 2 s. pres. m./p. ind. *or* subj. of κρατέω
    or 3 s. pres. act. subj. of κρατέω

18. 3 pl. aor. pass. subj. αἱρέω

19. 1 s. aor. act. subj. of μένω

20. 3 s. aor. act. subj. of παράγω
    or 2 s. aor. mid. subj. of παράγω

21. 3 pl. pres. m./p. ind. *or* subj. of ἡττάομαι

22. 1 pl. aor. act. subj. of ἀγγέλλω

23. 3 s. pres. m./p. subj. of αἱρέω

24. 3 s. aor. pass. subj. of ἀποδείκνυμι

25. 2 pl. pres. act. subj. of ἀκούω

26. 2 s. pres. act. subj. of ὑπομιμνῄσκω

27. 3 pl. pres. act. subj. of ἄπειμι (go away)

28. 1 pl. pres. m./p. subj. of ἁρπάζω

29. 3 s. aor. act. subj. of ἄρχω
    or 2 s. aor. mid. subj. of ἄρχω
    or 2 s. fut. mid. ind. of ἄρχω

30. 1 pl. aor. pass. subj. of τιμάω

31. 3 pl. pres. act. subj. of ἀφίστημι

32. 2 pl. aor. mid. subj. of δείκνυμι

33. 3 s. pres. m./p. subj. of ἡγέομαι

34. 2 pl. aor. act. subj. of ἐπιτρέπω

35. 1 s. aor. mid. subj. of πυνθάνομαι

36. 1 s. aor. pass. subj. of δηλόω

III.

1. μὴ προδῶτε τὴν ὑμετέραν πόλιν, ὦ ἄνδρες Ἀθηναῖοι.

2. φοβοῦνται μὴ οἱ παῖδες τοῖς δούλοις οὐ πιστεύωσιν (or πιστεύσωσιν).

3. βέλτιόν ἐστι τὴν θάλατταν τριήρων ἐμπλῆσαι ἵνα τὰς πολεμίας ναῦς τῇ πόλει ἐπιθέσθαι κωλύωμεν.

4. μηδεὶς μήποτε (or μήποτε μηδεὶς) ἡμᾶς ἐκείνων τῶν καιρῶν ἀναμνήσῃ (or ὑπομνήσῃ).

5. οὔποτε μὴ ἀποδείξῃς (or ἐπιδείξῃς) δικαιοτέρα οὖσα τῶν ἄλλων. or οὔποτε μὴ ἀποδείξῃς (or ἐπιδείξῃς) δικαιότερος ὢν τῶν ἄλλων.

6. πῶς ἀξίως τοῦτον ἐπαινέσω;

IV.

1. Whom am I to harm (*or* shall I harm) more justly than those who have wronged me?

2. The Greeks, having ceased to make war against each other, agree on a peace in order that the king may not easily conquer all.

3. Let us never be defeated by the female sex, since we are men.

4. Although we have exchanged [literally, *given and received*] a pledge, we are afraid that the Thebans may not be trustworthy.

5. If the city is not faring well, do not seem to be angry at those who are not to blame but rather at those who do not deliberate correctly.

6. While the cavalry was pursuing those who were fleeing, the general with the hoplites set up a trophy in order to demonstrate to all that his own army was better (*or* stronger) than the enemy's.

7. (Cf. Thuc. 7.8.2.) The general, fearing that those being sent might not report the true facts, himself wrote to the Assembly, for he hoped that in this way the Athenians would deliberate concerning the true state of affairs.

8. (Cf. Isaeus 8.4.) And now hear everything, in order that you not be ignorant of any of the things that happened but may know clearly about them.

9. (Cf. Isocr. 21.1.) I have come before you in order to speak on behalf of Isaeus. For he happens to be a friend to me, and in need, and being wronged, and unskilled at speaking, so that for all these reasons I have been persuaded to speak on his behalf.

10. (Cf. Isoc. 19.16.) So then, concerning the matter itself I believe that Callias has already made his presentation excellently; but in order that no one may suppose either that I accuse this man because of trivial causes or that he is worthy of gratitude from me, I want to speak on these topics.

V.

There still is left the puzzlement that you feel concerning good men: Why in the world do good men teach their own sons the other subjects that fall within the realm of teachers and make them wise (in these other subjects) but not make them [i.e., their sons] better than anyone (else) in that virtue in which they themselves are good? And on this question, Socrates, no longer shall I tell you a fable, but (instead) a reasoned account. For this is how one should think of it: Is there, or is there not, some one thing that it is necessary for all the citizens to partake of, if in fact there is going to be a city? For in this question is solved this puzzlement that you feel or nowhere else. For if there is (such a thing), then this one thing is not carpentry or bronzeworking or the art of ceramics, but rather righteousness, and self-control, and being pious. And taken all together I call it by a single name: a man's virtue.

UNIT THIRTY-THREE

I.

1. 1 s. aor. act. opt. of διαβαίνω
2. 3 pl. aor. act. subj. of ἐπαινέω
3. 1 pl. pres. m./p. subj. of ὁμολογέω
4. 1 pl. aor. act. opt. of ὑπομένω

5. 3 s. aor. act. opt. of ὑπολαμβάνω
6. 2 pl. aor. act. opt. of γιγνώσκω
7. 3 s. aor. act. opt. of ὑπακούω
8. aor. act. inf. of ὑπακούω

9. 2 pl. pres. act. subj. of δουλεύω

10. 2 s. aor. act. opt. of συμβουλεύω

11. 2 pl. aor. mid. opt. of συμφέρω

12. 3 pl. aor. mid. subj. of ἐπιτίθημι

13. 3 s. aor. mid. opt. of ἀποδίδωμι

14. 1 pl. pres. act. opt. of ἄπειμι (go away)

15. gen. s. f. pres. m./p. part. of ἀπολογέομαι

16. 3 s. aor. mid. opt. of ἀναιρέω

17. 1 s. aor. mid. opt. of ἀποκρίνω

18. 2 s. pres. act. subj. of διαβάλλω

19. 2 s. pres. m./p. opt. of δύναμαι

20. 3 s. impf. m./p. ind. of διαλέγομαι

21. 3 pl. fut. mid. ind. of ἐπιλανθάνομαι

22. nom. *or* voc. pl. f. pres. act. part. of καταλείπω

23. 2 s. aor. act. opt. of παραινέω

24. aor. act. inf. of συγγιγνώσκω

25. 3 s. aor. act. ind. of διαφέρω

26. 3 s. aor. act. opt. of ἀφίημι

27. 3 pl. aor. act. opt. of μεταδίδωμι

28. 1 pl. aor. act. subj. of φθάνω

29. 2 pl. fut. mid. opt. of τυγχάνω

30. 3 s. aor. act. opt. of τρέφω
   or aor. act. inf. of τρέφω
   or 2 s. aor. mid. impt. of τρέφω

31. 3 pl. pres. act. opt. of ποιέω

32. 2 s. pres. act. opt. of τιμάω

33. 3 s. pres. act. opt. of ἀδικέω

34. 1 pl. pres. act. opt. of ζηλόω

35. 2 pl. pres. act. opt. of πολεμέω

36. 3 s. fut. mid. opt. of πίπτω

37. 2 pl. pres. m./p. opt. of νικάω

38. 1 pl. pres. act. opt. of νοσέω

39. 3 pl. pres. m./p. opt. of χράομαι

II.

1. χρῆται

2. στρατεύοιεν

3. διαβληθεῖτε or διαβληθείητε

4. παραινέσοις

5. ὑπολάβοιμεν

6. ἀποκριναίμην

7. ἐφείης

8. χρήσαιντο

9. εἰδεῖεν or εἰδείησαν

10. συγγνοίητε (συγγνοῖτε not attested)

III.

1. μὴ σιγήσῃ.

2. ἴω ἢ μένω;

3. συμβουλευσώμεθα. or συμβουλευώμεθα.

4. μηδὲν ὑπόσχησθε. or μηδὲν ὑπόσχῃ.

5. σιγῶμεν ὅπως ὁ ποιητὴς τῶν κατηγορούντων διαφέρῃ ὡς κάλλιστα ἀπολογούμενος.

6. οἱ ἐμοὶ ἑταῖροι φοβοῦνται μὴ τῆς φιλίας ἐπιλαθόμενος διαβάλω or διαβάλλω αὐτούς.

IV.

1. At Pytho [i.e., Delphi] Apollo used to give (this) as an oracle to the Greeks: *Nothing in Excess.*

2. My father's friend, fearing because of his illness that he might leave his house to his enemies, made me his son [i.e., adopted me as his son].

3. (Cf. Isocr. 12.264.) The greater number of people were advising me to do what that man recommended.

4. (Cf. Isocr. 12.163.) Men of old understood that among wars the most just was the one that took place together with all men against the fearful strength of wild beasts and a second (just form of war) was that together with the Greeks against the Persians.

5. (Cf. Antiphon, *De Caede Herodis* 11.) The Athenians judge trials of murder under the sun, first in order that the jurymen not enter the same space as persons not pure in their hands, and second in order that the man prosecuting the case of murder not get too close to the murderer.

6. (Cf. Dem. 25.93.) Among other men we know that the best and most self-controlled are willing by their very nature to do all that is necessary *or* proper, while those who are inferior but not entirely wicked are prevented from erring by the fear they feel toward you.

V.

I, gentlemen, am, to be sure, delighted to be honored by you, if in fact I am human, and I feel gratitude and pray that the gods grant me the opportunity to show myself to be the cause of some good for you. On the other hand, for me to be chosen by you as leader in preference to a Lacedaemonian who is present does not seem to me to be advantageous to you, but it seems that you would less likely obtain (your request) because of this fact, if you should ask for anything from them [i.e., the Lacedaemonians]; and for me in turn I do not really think this is safe. For I observe that they [i.e., the Lacedaemonians] did not cease waging war against my country before they compelled the entire city to acknowledge that Lacedaemonians were their leaders too. . . . And as for the notion that you have in mind, namely that there would less (likely) be discord with one man leading than with many, know well that if you pick someone else, you will not find me engaging in dissension; for I believe that whoever while involved in a war foments dissension against a leader, this man stirs up trouble against his own safety. But if you chose me, perhaps you would find someone becoming angry both at you and at me.

UNIT THIRTY-FOUR

I.

1. 1 s. pres. act. opt. of ὁρμάω
2. 3 pl. pres. m./p. opt. of μισέω
3. acc. s. m. pres. act. part. of βοηθέω
   or nom. *or* acc. *or* voc. pl. n. pres.
   act. part. of βοηθέω
4. 3 s. pres. m./p. subj. of γαμέω
5. 2 s. pres. act. opt. of πολιορκέω
6. pres. act. inf. of ἀσθενέω
7. 2 s. pres. act. ind. *or* subj. of ἐρωτάω
8. 3 pl. pres. act. opt. of δαπανάω
9. nom. *or* voc. s. f. pres. act. part.
   of ζῶ
10. 1 pl. impf. act. ind. of ἀτιμάζω
11. 3 s. aor. act. opt. of γελάω
    or aor. act. inf. of γελάω

12. 1 pl. pres. act. opt. of ἀξιόω
13. pres. m./p. inf. of αἰτιάομαι
14. 3 pl. pres. act. ind. *or* subj. of ἐράω
    or dat. pl. m. *or* n. pres. act. part. of
    ἐράω
15. aor. mid. inf. of ἠρόμην (εἴρομαι)
16. 3 s. impf. act. ind. of ἐάω
17. 2 pl. aor. act. subj. of εὐεργετέω
18. 2 pl. fut. act. ind. of εὐεργετέω
19. 3 pl. aor. act. ind. of συγγιγνώσκω
20. 1 s. pres. m./p. opt. of ἀναιρέω
21. 1 s. impf. act. ind. of ἀπαντάω
    or 3 pl. impf. act. ind. of ἀπαντάω

II.

1. μισήσειαν *or* μισήσαιεν
2. γελασοίμην
3. γαμοῖσθε
4. ἀπαντῷεν *or* ἀπαντῴησαν
5. αἰτιασαίμεθα

6. ὁρμῷο
7. τελέσαιτο
8. αἰτήσαιμεν
9. ἐρῴη *or* ἐρῷ
10. ἀτιμάζοις

III.

1. ἀφικόμενος δὲ τοὺς Ἀθηναίους ἤγγειλε μισήσαντας τοὺς μὴ βοηθοῦντας τοῖς
   ἀσθενέσιν.
   or ἀφικόμενος δὲ ἤγγειλε ὅτι οἱ Ἀθηναῖοι τοὺς μὴ βοηθοῦντας τοῖς ἀσθενέσι
   μισήσειαν.
   or ἀφικόμενος δὲ ἤγγειλε ὅτι οἱ Ἀθηναῖοι τοὺς μὴ βοηθοῦντας τοῖς ἀσθενέσιν
   ἐμίσησαν.
2. ὁ βασιλεὺς ἐφοβεῖτο μὴ ὁ Κῦρος τοῖς ἄλλοις στρατηγοῖς ἐπιβουλεύοι· ὥστε
   παρεκελεύσατο αὐτοῖς φυλάττεσθαι.
   or ὁ βασιλεὺς ἐφοβεῖτο μὴ ὁ Κῦρος τοῖς ἄλλοις στρατηγοῖς ἐπιβουλεύῃ· ὥστε
   παρεκελεύσατο αὐτοῖς φυλάττεσθαι.
3. μήποτε ἐπιλάθοιο. τοῦτο δοῖεν οἱ θεοί.

4. εἴθε τὸ στράτευμα παρῆν. αὔριον ἀφίκοιτο.

5. αὔριον πευσόμεθα (or μαθησόμεθα) ποῦ τοῖς συμμάχοις ἡμῶν ἀπαντησόμεθα.

6. ἅμα τῇ ἡμέρᾳ σχεδὸν πάντες οἱ ἱππῆς πρὸς τὴν θάλατταν ὥρμησαν (or ὡρμήσαντο), φανερὸν (or δῆλον) ὂν ὅτι οὐδεὶς ἀξιοῖ (or ἀξιοίη) τοὺς πολεμίους αἰσθέσθαι ἐὰν ὅ τι οἱ πολῖται παρεσκευάσαντο (or παρασκευάσαιντο).
or ἅμα τῇ ἡμέρᾳ σχεδὸν πάντες οἱ ἱππῆς πρὸς τὴν θάλατταν ὥρμησαν (or ὡρμήσαντο), οὐδενὸς φανεροῦ (or δήλου) ὄντος ἀξιοῦντος τοὺς πολεμίους αἰσθέσθαι ἐὰν ὅ τι οἱ πολῖται παρεσκευάσαντο (or παρασκευάσαιντο).

IV.

1. When the young man asked which of the three daughters it was advantageous to marry, we replied with a laugh that we did not know.

2. Are we to permit the king to continue besieging the town, or are we to go to the rescue?

3. (Cf. Andocides, *Myst.* 117.) Listen, gentlemen (for perhaps you would want to learn it): With what intention (*or* Wanting what) did Callias do those things?

4. The soldiers kept asking how they were to benefit Cyrus, since it was not possible to carry out a campaign without money. For they did not think it proper to obey a general who was spending less than he promised.

5. (Cf. Antiphon, *De Caede Herodis* 71.) And this perhaps would become clear later on, in what manner the fellow was dishonored.

6. To those from Croesus who were asking for an oracle the god replied as follows: "It is necessary for Croesus to destroy a great empire if he crosses the Halys River." And having heard this Croesus thought that he himself would conquer his enemies, not interpreting well. And not fearing that he might be making a mistake in trusting his own judgment, he went on campaign against the Persians in order that after defeating these people he might rule all of Asia. But things turned out otherwise. For the Lydians were conquered, and Croesus and his wife and children were captured. And when captured he said this to himself: "I wish that I had never crossed the Halys. And now what are we to suffer? Are we to be slaves to the Persians? It is not a terrible thing for people in misfortune to die, but may the Persians not cut off my head."

V.

After this it was very obvious that his fellow ambassadors were vexed at Hecatonymus because of what had been said, and another of them stepped forward and said that they had come not to make war but to demonstrate that they are friends. "And if you come to the city of the Sinopeans, we will receive (you) there with gifts of hospitality, but for now we will order the people here to give what they can. For we see that everything that you say is true." After this the Cotyoritans were sending guest-gifts, and the generals of the Greeks were entertaining the ambassadors of the Sinopeans, and they had many friendly conversations with each other, both on other topics and they inquired in detail concerning the remaining journey about those things that each of the two groups needed. On that day this end result came about. And on the next day the generals gathered their soldiers. And it seemed best to them to deliberate concerning the rest of the journey, after first summoning the Sinopeans (to join them in the discussion).

UNIT THIRTY-FIVE

I.

1. οἱ ἄνδρες οὕστινας διαλεγόμενος ὁ Σωκράτης ἐλέγχοι τοῖς παροῦσιν ἐφαίνοντο μηδὲν εἰδέναι, ὥστε αὐτῷ ὠργίζοντο.
2. ἐὰν αὐτῶν κατηγορήσωμεν, οὐ ῥᾳδίως ἡμῖν ὁμολογήσουσιν.
3. ἐπειδὰν ὁ πρέσβυς ἔλθῃ, τοῦτο ἐρήσεσθε (or ἐρωτήσετε) ἢ οὔ;
4. εἰ τὰ ὅπλα καὶ τὰ πλοῖα καταλιπόντες αὐτίκα φύγοιεν, οὐδὲν ἂν εἴη θαῦμα.
5. μείζων ἂν ἦν ὁ κίνδυνος εἰ μὴ τῆς νυκτὸς ἤλασαν or ἐπορεύθησαν.

II.

1. Whoever treats ambassadors unjustly pays the penalty, if not immediately, at least in the end.
2. If without being noticed the three brothers steal the weapons that the Thebans dedicated, they will become rich although they have done impious things.
3. At Athens in the old days the jurymen were admired who cast their vote in accordance with justice and the laws after hearing the speeches of both sides.
4. If you should run very swiftly, perhaps you would escape the danger.
5. In return for these things, whatever benefactions they might do now, they would get back gratitude both while alive and after the end of their lives.
6. If the young man spends a lot because he is in love with the courtesan, it will not be good for his household, since it is already lacking in money.
7. It is fitting always to do whatever the wise recommend.
8. (Cf. Plato, *Apol.* 25a.) Do all Athenians except me, then, as you claim, make the young good and noble, and I alone make them worse?
9. (Cf. Xen. *Hell.* 6.5.15.) If the fifty cavalrymen had not prevented it, the Lacedaemonians would have crossed into this land and made camp beneath the mountains to the west of the city.

10. (Cf. Plato, *Parm.* 126a.) After I arrived at Athens, I met with Adeimantus and Glaucon in the marketplace. And Adeimantus, taking hold of my hand, said, "Greetings, Cephalus, and if you have need of anything of the things here that we can do, tell (us)." I said, "But I am here for just this purpose, to make a request of you."

III.

[Socrates] Indeed wondering at these (very) things, Gorgias, I have been asking for some time now what in the world the power of the art of rhetoric is. For it appears to *me* as quite miraculous in its magnitude, when I consider it this way.

[Gorgias] Yes, Socrates, (you certainly would call it miraculous) if you should know all the facts, namely that so to speak it encompasses and controls under itself all the powers. And I'll tell you an important piece of evidence. For *I* have often in the past, when visiting with my brother or with the other physicians one of the sick who is not willing to drink a drug or to allow the physician to cut or burn [i.e., do surgery or cautery], though the physician was unable to persuade (the patient), *I* persuaded him, using no other craft than the art of rhetoric. And I also maintain that if a rhetorically skilled man and a physician went to a city, wherever you want, if it should be necessary for them to compete in speech in an assembly or in some other gathering as to which of the two ought to be chosen [i.e., elected] as physician, then the physician would make no showing at all, but the man who is able to speak would be chosen, if he should want to be. And if he should compete against any *other* skilled craftsman at all, the rhetorically skilled man would persuade (the Assembly) to select him rather (*or* more easily) than any other person would. For there is nothing about which the rhetorically skilled man would not speak more persuasively than any other of the skilled craftsmen before a crowd.

IV.

[Chremylos]
I (*or* I for one) believe that this is clear to understand for all men equally,
that it is just for the good among men to fare well,
and for the wicked and godless to fare, surely, the opposite of this.
So then, longing for (this), with difficulty have we discovered this, a way so that there arises
a plan fine and noble and useful for every purpose.
For if Wealth *now* gets his sight and does not go around being blind,
he will make his way to the good among men and will not leave them,
but the wicked and godless he will avoid. And then he will cause

all men to be good and certainly rich and reverent toward divine things.

And yet who could ever discover anything better than this for mankind?

[Blepsidemos]

No one could; I serve as your witness for this fact; don't ask *her* at all.

[Chremylos]

For as life is now disposed for us humans,

who would not believe that it is madness and, even more than that, accursed
   misfortune?

For many among mortals who are wicked are wealthy,

having collected their possessions unjustly; and many who are altogether virtuous

are suffering bad fortune and are starving and for the most part spend their life
   with you [Poverty].

UNIT THIRTY-SIX

I.

1. οὐκ ἐχρῆν (or ἔδει) τοὺς νόμους προδιδόναι, ὦ ἄνδρες δικασταί.

2. ἑάλωσαν ἂν εἴκοσιν ὁπλῖται ἐκείνῃ τῇ ἡμέρᾳ εἰ μὴ οἱ φυγάδες (or οἱ
   φεύγοντες) ἐβοήθησαν.

3. εἰ μὴ οἱ φύλακες ἐν τῷ ἱερῷ τῆς νυκτὸς παρῆσαν, οἱ χρημάτων ἀποροῦντες
   πάντα ταχέως ἂν ἔκλεπτον.

4. ἐὰν οἱ ἀδελφοὶ ἐν τῇ μάχῃ ἀλλήλοις ἀπαντῶσι, πότερος πότερον ἀποκτενεῖ;

II.

1. Everyone should have fought even on behalf of the Thebans if the foreigners
   had besieged their city.

2. Then no one would have taken bribes from the enemy, but now every single
   man, surely, seeks to become a traitor.

3. The citizens were suffering terrible things. For in fact the women, leaving
   their children and husbands at home, were running to the mountain, different women from different directions (*or* some from one direction, some from
   another).

4. (Plato, *Phaedrus* 227a.) My dear Phaedrus, where (are you going) and from
   where (are you coming)? —From Lysias the son of Cephalus, Socrates, and I
   am going for a walk outside the city wall.

5. (Plato, *Phaedrus* 237b–c.) On every subject, child, there is a single (proper)
   beginning for those who are going to deliberate well: one must know that

concerning which the deliberation is (taking place), or else one must miss the entire goal.

6. (Cf. Xen. *Anab.* 6.6.17–19.) I did this at the order neither of Xenophon nor of anyone else. But when I saw a good man, one of my fellow soldiers, being led (along) by Dexippus, whom *you* know betrayed you, it seemed terrible to me. And I took the man away (from Dexippus) by force, I admit it.

7. (Cf. Dem. 19.302.) For you would correctly get angry, men of Athens, at every man doing so many (*or* so great) evils, but not, however, at anyone more, or more justly, than at this fellow.

8. (Cf. Isaeus 8.5.) It is, to be sure, a difficult thing, gentlemen, to be put into a judicial contest concerning such matters with these men, who are not speaking true things, when one is entirely inexperienced in court cases. Despite that, I have many hopes that I will in fact receive just treatment from you.

9. (Cf. Lysias 29.21.) For these reasons, having left aside the discussion concerning myself, I want to recall the life of Alcibiades. And yet I am really at a loss (from) where I am to begin because of the large number of his unjust deeds.

10. (Cf. Andoc. *Alcib.* 10.) Having come to trust Callias, she gave him certain money for her own burial, but not to this man, though he is her own son. Isn't it indeed clear that she knew well that he would not do what was required?

III.

I would consider it of great importance, gentlemen, that you should show yourselves to be for me exactly the sorts of judges concerning this affair that you would be for yourselves if you had suffered such treatment. For I know full well that if you should hold the very same opinion concerning other men as you do concerning yourselves, there would not be anyone who would fail to be vexed at the things that occurred; rather you would all consider the penalties applying to those who practice such behavior small. And these matters would not be judged thus only among you, but in all of Greece. For concerning this crime alone both under a democracy and under an oligarchy the same right to vengeance has been granted to the weakest citizens against those who have the greatest power, so that the lowliest man receives the same rights as the noblest. To such a degree, gentlemen, do all men consider this (form of) insolence most dreadful. Now then, as far as the magnitude of the penalty is concerned, I believe that you all hold the same notion, and that no one is of such a careless disposition that he [literally, *who*] believes those who are responsible for such deeds ought to receive pardon or deems them worthy of a small penalty.

UNIT THIRTY-SEVEN

I.

1. 3 pl. perf. act. ind. of ὄμνυμι
2. perf. act. inf. of ῥίπτω
3. nom. *or* acc. *or* voc. s. n. perf. act. part. of συμβαίνω
4. 2 pl. perf. act. ind. of ἀκούω
5. acc. s. m. perf. (2) act. part. of ἀπόλλυμι
   nom. *or* acc. *or* voc. pl. n. perf. (2) act. part. of ἀπόλλυμι
6. acc. s. f. perf. (1) act. part. of ἀπόλλυμι
7. 1 pl. perf. act. ind. of βλάπτω
8. 3 s. perf. act. ind. of φεύγω
9. dat. s. m. *or* n. perf. act. part. of λανθάνω
10. perf. act. inf. of τάττω
11. 3 pl. plup. act. ind. of σπουδάζω
12. 1 pl. (masc.) perf. (2) act. subj. of ἀπόλλυμι
13. 3 s. (fem.) fut. perf. act. ind. of ῥίπτω
14. nom. *or* acc. *or* voc. s. n. perf. act. part. of μανθάνω
15. perf. act. inf. of πράττω
16. dat. p. m. *or* n. perf. act. part. of πίνω
17. gen. pl. f. perf. act. part. of ἐσθίω
18. 2 s. perf. act. ind. of φαίνω
19. perf. act. inf. of ἔρχομαι
20. 1 s. pluperf. act. ind. of βαίνω
21. perf. act. inf. of πέμπω
22. 1 pl. perf. act. ind. of πάσχω
23. 1 s. perf. act. ind. of νομίζω
24. 3 pl. perf. act. ind. of θαυμάζω
25. 1 s. perf. act. ind. of ἐρέω
26. 3 s. pluperf. act. ind. of ὄμνυμι
27. 2 s. aor. act. impt. of γιγνώσκω
28. 2 s. pluperf. act. ind. of ἀκούω

II.

1. ἔρριφας or βέβληκας
2. ἐτετιμήκεμεν
3. μεμισηκέναι
4. ἠξιώκασι(ν)
5. ἡρπάκατε
6. ἡμαρτηκέναι
7. ἐκεκλήκει(ν)
8. ηὑρηκότες
9. μεμαθήκοι or μεμαθηκὼς εἴη or μεμαθηκυῖα εἴη
10. προδεδωκυίαις
11. κεκωλύκοιμι or κεκωλυκυῖα εἴην
12. διεγνωκότας

III.

I believe, gentlemen, that I must demonstrate this fact, that Eratosthenes committed adultery with my wife and both corrupted her and shamed my children and wantonly insulted me myself, coming into my house, and that there was no enmity between me and him except for this one, nor did I do this for the sake of money, in order to become rich instead of poor, nor for the sake of any other profit except the retribution provided for by the laws. Well then, I shall show to you all of my own affairs from the beginning, leaving nothing out, but telling the true facts. For I believe this course is my only means of safety, if I prove able to tell you all the things that have been done. For, Athenians, when I decided to marry and took a wife into my house, for the [literally, *other*] whole earlier period of time I was so disposed that neither did I vex (my wife) nor was it too much in her own power to do whatever she wanted, and I kept guarding her as much as was possible and I paid attention, just as was reasonable. But when a child was born to me, from that time I trusted her and turned over all my [household] affairs to her, believing that this [i.e., the birth of our child] was the greatest bond of intimacy.

UNIT THIRTY-EIGHT

I.

1. 3 pl. pluperf. act. ind. of ἀθροίζω
2. 2 s. pluperf. m./p. ind. of δείκνυμι
3. nom. *or* voc. pl. m. perf. m./p. part. of μιμνήσκω
4. 3 s. perf. m./p. ind. of κρύπτω
5. 2 pl. perf. m./p. ind. of διαλέγομαι *or* 2 pl. pluperf. m./p. ind. of διαλέγομαι
6. 3 s. perf. m./p. ind. of φυλάττω
7. nom. *or* acc. *or* voc. pl. n. perf. m./p. part. of δοκέω
8. 3 pl. perf. m./p. ind. of κτάομαι
9. 2 s. perf. m./p. ind. of τάττω
10. 2 s. fut. perf. m./p. ind. of μιμνήσκω
11. acc. pl. m. perf. m./p. part. of τιμάω
12. perf. m./p. inf. of καλέω
13. 1 pl. perf. m./p. ind. of τρέφω
14. 3 pl. (neut.) pluperf. m./p. ind. of πράττω
15. perf. m./p. inf. of τρέπω
16. 3 pl. perf. act. ind. of τίθημι
17. 1 pl. perf. m./p. ind. of πυνθάνομαι
18. gen. s. m. *or* n. perf. m./p. part. of ὀργίζομαι
19. gen. pl. f. perf. act. part. of ἔρχομαι
20. 3 s. fut. perf. m./p. ind. of καλέω
21. 3 pl. (fem.) perf. m./p. subj. of πιστεύω
22. 2 pl. perf. *or* pluperf. m./p. ind. of σπένδω
23. 3 pl. perf. m./p. opt. of κτάομαι
24. perf. m./p. inf. of τέμνω
25. 1 pl. perf. *or* pluperf. m./p. ind. of ἡττάομαι
26. 3 s. pluperf. m./p. ind. of ἐλέγχω
27. 3 pl. (fem.) fut. perf. m./p. ind. of γυμνάζω
28. 1 s. fut. perf. m./p. ind. of παύω

II.

1. ἔρριφθε or ἐβέβλησθε
2. τετιμήμεθα
3. ὦφθαι or ἑωρᾶσθαι
4. μεμνησόμεθα
5. ἡρπασμέναι ὦσι
6. πεφοβῆσθαι
7. κέκληται
8. πεπόμφῃς or πεπομφὼς ᾖς or πεπομφυῖα ᾖς
9. ἤγγελτο
10. προδεδομένη
11. κεκομισμένοι εἶμεν or εἴημεν
12. γεγενημένα

III.

1.

αἱρεῖ	αἱρήσει	εἷλε	ᾕρηκε
αἱρῇ		ἕλῃ	ᾑρήκῃ or ᾑρηκὼς (-κυῖα) ᾖ
αἱροίη or αἱροῖ	αἱρήσοι	ἕλοι	ᾑρήκοι or ᾑρηκὼς (-κυῖα) εἴη
αἱρεῖν	αἱρήσειν	ἑλεῖν	ᾑρηκέναι
αἱρῶν	αἱρήσων	ἑλών	ᾑρηκώς
ᾕρει			ᾑρήκει(ν)
			ᾑρηκὼς (-κυῖα) ἔσται
αἱρεῖται	αἱρήσεται	εἵλετο	ᾕρηται
αἱρῆται		ἕληται	ᾑρημένος (-μένη, -μένον) ᾖ
αἱροῖτο	αἱρήσοιτο	ἕλοιτο	ᾑρημένος (-μένη, -μένον) εἴη
αἱρεῖσθαι	αἱρήσεσθαι	ἑλέσθαι	ᾑρῆσθαι
αἱρούμενος	αἱρησόμενος	ἑλόμενος	ᾑρημένος
ᾑρεῖτο			ᾕρητο
			ᾑρήσεται or ᾑρημένος (-μένη, -μένον) ἔσται
			ᾑρήσεσθαι
	αἱρεθήσεται	ᾑρέθη	
		αἱρεθῇ	
	αἱρεθήσοιτο	αἱρεθείη	
	αἱρεθήσεσθαι	αἱρεθῆναι	
	αἱρεθησόμενος	αἱρεθείς	

2.

τίθετε	θήσετε	ἔθετε	τεθήκατε
τιθῆτε		θῆτε	τεθήκητε or τεθηκότες (-κυῖαι) ἦτε
τιθεῖτε or τιθείητε	θήσοιτε	θεῖτε or θείητε	τεθήκοιτε or τεθηκότες (-κυῖαι) εἴητε (εἶτε)
τίθετε		θέτε	τεθηκότες ἔστε
τιθέναι	θήσειν	θεῖναι	τεθηκέναι
τιθείς	θήσων	θείς	τεθηκώς
ἐτίθετε			ἐτεθήκετε
			τεθηκότες (-κυῖαι) ἔσεσθε
τίθεσθε	θήσεσθε	ἔθεσθε	τέθεισθε
τιθῆσθε		θῆσθε	τεθειμένοι (-μέναι) ἦτε
τιθεῖσθε	θήσοισθε	θεῖσθε	τεθειμένοι (-μέναι) εἴητε (or εἶτε)
τίθεσθε		θέσθε	τεθειμένοι (-μέναι) ἔστε
τίθεσθαι	θήσεσθαι	θέσθαι	τεθεῖσθαι
τιθέμενος	θησόμενος	θέμενος	τεθειμένος

ἐτίθεσθε

ἐτέθεισθε
τεθείσεσθε or τεθειμένοι
   (-μέναι) ἔσεσθε
τεθείσεσθαι

τεθήσεσθε

ἐτέθητε
τεθῆτε

τεθήσοισθε

τεθείητε or τεθεῖτε
τέθητε

τεθήσεσθαι

τεθῆναι

τεθησόμενος

τεθείς

3.

ῥίπτουσι	ῥίψουσι	ἔρριψαν	ἐρρίφασι
ῥίπτωσι		ῥίψωσι	ἐρρίφωσι or ἐρριφότες (-φυῖαι) ὦσι
ῥίπτοιεν	ῥίψοιεν	ῥίψαιεν or ῥίψειαν	ἐρρίφοιεν or ἐρριφότες (-φυῖαι) εἶεν (or εἴησαν)
ῥίπτειν	ῥίψειν	ῥῖψαι	ἐρριφέναι
ῥίπτων	ῥίψων	ῥίψας	ἐρριφώς
ἔρριπτον			ἐρρίφεσαν
			ἐρριφότες (-φυῖαι) ἔσονται
ῥίπτονται	ῥίψονται	ἐρρίψαντο	ἐρριμμένοι (-μέναι) εἰσί
ῥίπτωνται		ῥίψωνται	ἐρριμμένοι (-μέναι) ὦσι
ῥίπτοιντο	ῥίψοιντο	ῥίψαιντο	ἐρριμμένοι (-μέναι) εἶεν (or εἴησαν)
ῥίπτεσθαι	ῥίψεσθαι	ῥίψασθαι	ἐρρῖφθαι
ῥιπτόμενος	ῥιψόμενος	ῥιψάμενος	ἐρριμμένος
ἐρρίπτοντο			ἐρριμμένοι (-μέναι) ἦσαν
			ἐρρίψονται or ἐρριμμένοι (-μέναι) ἔσονται
			ἐρρίψεσθαι
	ῥιφθήσονται or ῥιφήσονται	ἐρρίφθησαν or ἐρρίφησαν	
		ῥιφθῶσι or ῥιφῶσι	
	ῥιφθήσοιντο or ῥιφήσοιντο	ῥιφθεῖεν or ῥιφθείησαν or ῥιφεῖεν or ῥιφείησαν	
	ῥιφθήσεσθαι or ῥιφήσεσθαι	ῥιφθῆναι or ῥιφῆναι	
	ῥιφθησόμενος or ῥιφησόμενος	ῥιφθείς or ῥιφείς	

4.

βουλεύομεν	βουλεύσομεν	ἐβουλεύσαμεν	βεβουλεύκαμεν
βουλεύωμεν		βουλεύσωμεν	βεβουλεύκωμεν or
			βεβουλευκότες (-κυῖαι) ὦμεν
βουλεύοιμεν	βουλεύσοιμεν	βουλεύσαιμεν	βεβουλεύκοιμεν or
			βεβουλευκότες (-κυῖαι)
			εἶμεν (or εἴημεν)
βουλεύειν	βουλεύσειν	βουλεῦσαι	βεβουλευκέναι
βουλεύων	βουλεύσων	βουλεύσας	βεβουλευκώς
ἐβουλεύομεν			ἐβεβουλεύκεμεν
			βεβουλευκότες (-κυῖαι)
			ἐσόμεθα
βουλευόμεθα	βουλευσόμεθα	ἐβουλευσάμεθα	βεβουλεύμεθα
βουλευώμεθα		βουλευσώμεθα	βεβουλευμένοι (-μέναι) ὦμεν
βουλευοίμεθα	βουλευσοίμεθα	βουλευσαίμεθα	βεβουλευμένοι (-μέναι) εἶμεν
			(or εἴημεν)
βουλεύεσθαι	βουλεύσεσθαι	βουλεύσασθαι	βεβουλεῦσθαι
βουλευόμενος	βουλευσόμενος	βουλευσάμενος	βεβουλευμένος
ἐβουλευόμεθα			ἐβεβουλεύμεθα
			βεβουλεύσονται or
			βεβουλευμένοι (-μέναι)
			ἐσόμεθα
	βουλευθησόμεθα	ἐβουλεύθημεν	
		βουλευθῶμεν	
	βουλευθησοίμεθα	βουλευθείημεν or	
		βουλευθεῖμεν	
	βουλευθήσεσθαι	βουλευθῆναι	
	βουλευθησόμενος	βουλευθείς	

IV.

(1) καὶ μηδεὶς ὑμῶν ἡμᾶς τοὺς Ἕλληνας νομίσῃ κάκιον ἔχειν ὅτι οἱ τοῦ Κύρου στρατιῶται, καίπερ πρόσθεν σὺν ἡμῖν ταττόμενοι, νῦν ἀφεστήκασιν. (2) οὗτοι γὰρ ἔτι κακίονές (or κακίους) εἰσι τῶν ὑφ᾿ ἡμῶν ἡττημένων. (3) καταλιπόντες γὰρ ἡμᾶς ἐκείνους ἔφυγον. (4) πολὺ δὲ κρεῖττον (or βέλτιον or ἄμεινον) τοὺς ἐθέλοντας φυγῆς ἄρχειν σὺν τοῖς πολεμίοις ταττομένους ὁρᾶν ἢ ἐν τῇ ἡμετέρᾳ τάξει. (5) καὶ μὴ φοβηθῆτε τοὺς τῶν πολεμίων ἱππέας, καίπερ πολλοὺς ὄντας.

V.

Now then, the truth is like this, and you will recognize it, if you move on to more important things, finally leaving aside philosophy. For, you know, Socrates, philoso-phy is a charming thing, if one touches upon it in moderation in the prime of one's youth. But if one spends one's time in it farther along than is proper, it is the ruination of men. For if one is indeed very greatly innately gifted and practices philosophy far along in one's prime, one inevitably turns out to be inexperienced in all the things in which the man who is going to be noble-and-good and famous must be experienced. For indeed such men become inexperienced in the laws that operate in the city, and in the speeches that one must use when associating with one's fellow men in contractual transactions both in private life and in public, and in the pleasures and desires that are human, and to sum it up, they become completely inexperienced in human behavior. So whenever they become involved in some private or civic activity, they turn out to be ridiculous, exactly as, I suppose, the politically savvy, when in turn they get involved in your pastimes and discussions, are ridiculous.

UNIT THIRTY-NINE

I.

1. nom. *or* voc. pl. f. aor. pass. part. of τίθημι
2. 2 pl. fut. pass. ind. of ἥδομαι
3. 2 pl. perf. (2) *or* pluperf. (2) act. ind. of καθίστημι
4. 2 s. aor. pass. opt. of ῥήγνυμι
5. nom. s. m. fut. pass. part. of κρίνω
6. 3 s. fut. mid. opt. of τρέχω
7. nom. *or* acc. *or* voc. s. n. aor. pass. part. of ὁμολογέω
8. 3 pl. perf. (2) act. ind. of δέδια *or* δέδοικα
9. 3 s. pres. act. impt. of ὑποπτεύω
10. 2 s. pres. act. impt. of φράζω
11. aor. act. inf. of ἀπέχω
12. 3 pl. perf. m./p. subj. of κτάομαι
13. 1 s. aor. act. subj. of λανθάνω
14. 1 pl. perf. (2) act. ind. of ἀποθνῄσκω
15. 2 pl. fut. mid. ind. of βουλεύω
16. 2 s. aor. pass. impt. of μιμνῄσκω
17. 3 s. aor. act. impt. of διώκω
18. 2 pl. pres. act. ind. *or* impt. of σκοπέω
19. 2 s. pres. act. impt. of ἐπιχειρέω
20. 3 s. impf. act. ind. of ἐπιχειρέω
21. 2 pl. pres. act. impt. of εἶμι
22. 3 pl. (masc.) perf. act. impt. of ὁμολογέω
23. aor. act. inf. of βουλεύω
24. 3 pl. perf. act. ind. of πειράω
25. 2 s. aor. act. opt. of νικάω
26. 2 s. aor. mid. impt. of ἄγω
27. 3 pl. pres. act. impt. of ἐξαπατάω *or* gen. pl. m. *or* n. pres. act. part. of ἐξαπατάω
28. 2 s. aor. act. impt. of καταλείπω
29. 2 pl. aor. mid. impt. of σκέπτομαι
30. dat. s. m. *or* n. perf. act. part. of παύω
31. 3 pl. (fem.) perf. m./p. ind. of ἐλέγχω
32. 2 s. aor. act. impt. of κατατίθημι
33. 3 s. (neut.) perf. m./p. impt. of τελέω

II.

1. (Cf. Plato, *Phaedo* 91c.) You must be careful that I do not, by being too eager, deceive myself and you at the same time.

2. (Cf. Thuc. 1.57.) Demosthenes, after sinking the triremes of the enemy, left the other general on the land, having urged him to keep guard over the nearby cities to see that they do not revolt.

3. (Cf. Thuc. 1.82.) If we set our hands to the war immediately, consider how we will not fare in a way unworthy of our fatherland.

4. (Cf. Isocr. 17.18.) I ordered him to find a way, by whatever means he wants, that both for this man things will be fine and I will recover my own property.

5. (Cf. Isocr. 4.172.) The more wicked the public speakers actually are, the more the others must look out for how we will dissolve the existing hatred.

6. (Cf. Isoc. 7.33.) For they were not afraid that they might suffer the one or the other of two things, (namely that) either they might be deprived of (*or* lose) everything or, after getting a lot of troublesome business, they might recover (only) a small portion of what had been given freely.

7. (Andoc. *De Pace* 28.) Now then, I am most afraid of that aspect, men of Athens—the accustomed evil—that we always let go of our better friends and choose the worse ones, and that we make war on account of other people, when it is possible for us to be at peace on our own account.

8. (Cf. ps.-Dem. 52.14.) When he perceived that his father was already in a disabled condition and was with difficulty making his way up to town and that his eye was failing him, he forced him into a lawsuit and made terrible accusations.

9. (Cf Plato, *Symp.* 175a.) Just now Socrates was coming in behind me; but I myself also am wondering where he might be.

10. (Cf. Xen. *Hell.* 4.4.9.) Having seen the great number of the enemy, they seemed to themselves to be (too) few, so that they built in front of themselves a wall of the (best) sort they could.

III.

For there was once a time when the gods existed, but mortal species did not exist. And when the fated time of birth came for these too, the gods mold them inside the earth combining them out of earth and fire and those things however many are blended with earth and fire. And when they were about to lead them toward the light, they assigned to Prometheus and Epimetheus the task of adorning and distributing faculties to each group as is proper. Epimetheus asks Prometheus as a favor that he himself do the distributing, "and after I have distributed," he said, "inspect (my work)." And thus persuading him [i.e., Prometheus] he [i.e., Epimetheus] apportions. And in apportioning he attached to some strength without swiftness, but the weaker creatures he equipped with swiftness. . . . Now since he was not really very smart, Epimetheus did not realize that he had used up the faculties on the brute animals. Now the human race still remained for him unequipped, and he was at a loss as to how he was to deal with the situation. And while he is in this puzzlement, Prometheus comes to him to inspect the distribution, and he sees that all the other animals are suitably provided with everything, but mankind is naked and without covering for the feet and without bedding and without armor. And already the fated day was present on which mankind too had to go out of the earth into the light.

UNIT FORTY

I.

1. (Cf. Xen. *Cyrop.* 7.1.10.) Do you realize, gentlemen, that the present contest concerns not only your victory today but also the previous victory that you have won and your prosperity as a whole?
2. (Cf. Xen. *Cyrop.* 7.1.11.) Men, from this point on, it will no longer be necessary (*or* proper) ever to hold the gods to blame for anything at all: for they have handed over to us many fine things to acquire. But let us show that we are brave men.
3. (Cf. Isocr. 9.80.) So then, it is my task and that of your other friends to say and write such things by means of which we are likely to persuade you to aim for these very things that even now you actually do desire; and it falls to you (*or* belongs to you *or* behooves you) to leave nothing undone, but, just as in the present, also for the future time to take care and to exercise your soul to make sure that you will be worthy of your father and your brothers.

II.

So then, gripped by doubt as to what salvation he was to find for mankind, Prometheus steals the artistic skill of Hephaestus and Athena together with fire—for it was impossible for it [i.e., this artistic skill] to become capable of being possessed by anyone or useful to anyone without fire—and thus indeed he makes a gift (of them) to mankind. Now then, although man obtained in this way the skill concerned with (the maintenance of) life, he did not have political skill. For this was at Zeus's side. . . . And since mankind partook of a divine portion, first, because of his kinship with the divine, he alone of animals believed in the gods, and he attempted to found altars and images of the gods; second, he quickly articulated the sound of the voice and words by the use of art, and he discovered for himself dwellings and forms of clothing and footwear and forms of bedding and nourishment from the earth. Equipped, then, like this, in the beginning people used to live scattered here and there, and there were no cities. Therefore they used to be destroyed by the wild beasts because they were weaker than the animals in all respects, and the craftsmen's art was a sufficient helper for them with regard to nourishment, but with regard to the war of the wild beasts it was deficient—for they did not yet have political skill, a part of which is the art of warfare—thus they used to seek to gather themselves together and to preserve themselves by founding cities. Whenever, then, they were gathered together, they used to wrong each other because they did not have the political skill, so that again they were scattered and kept being destroyed.

III.

Being in such a predicament I decided to take a risk, since being put to death was already close to hand. And after summoning Damnippus I say this to him: "You happen to be a close acquaintance of mine, and I have now come into your house, and I am guilty of no wrong but am being destroyed for the sake of money. You, therefore, furnish to me, who am suffering these things, your own power eagerly disposed toward my salvation." And he promised that he would do this. But it seemed better to him to make mention of it to Theognis. For he believed that he [i.e., Theognis] would do anything if someone would offer him money. And while that man was conversing with Theognis (since I happened to be knowledgeable about the house and I knew that it had a door at either end), I decided to try to save myself by that way, considering that, if I get away unseen, I would be saved, while if I get caught, I believed that, on the one hand, if Theognis should have been persuaded by Damnippus to accept money, I would be let go nonetheless, and on the other hand, if not [i.e., if Theognis had not agreed], I was going to die all the same.

UNIT FORTY-ONE

I.

1. perf. (1) act. inf. of δέδοικα
2. acc. s. f. perf. act. part. of ἐπιστέλλω
3. 2 pl. aor. mid. subj. of ἀλλάττω
4. aor. act. inf. of ἀφίημι
5. 3 s. pluperf. m./p. ind. of ἐργάζομαι
6. nom. *or* acc. *or* voc. pl. n. perf. m./p. part. of γράφω
7. 3 s. perf. act. ind. of φύω
8. 2 s. perf. act. ind. of ἔοικα
9. perf. (2) act. inf. of ἀφίστημι
10. 3 s. pres. m./p. ind. of διανοέομαι
11. 2 s. pres. act. impt. of χαίρω
12. 3 s. fut. mid. ind. of ἀποπλέω
13. 3 pl. (neut.) pluperf. m./p. ind. of ἐργάζομαι
14. 1 pl. aor. act. ind. of φύω
15. 1 pl. perf. act. ind. of ἔοικα
16. 3 s. aor. (1) act. impt. of καθίστημι
17. 3 pl. perf. (2) act. ind. of (ἀπο)θνῄσκω
18. nom. *or* voc. s. f. aor. pass. part. of ἀλλάττω

II.

1. ὁ Κῦρος στρατιώτας καὶ χρήματα ἀθροίζων διετέλει ἕως ὁ βασιλεὺς τὸν ἀδελφόν τι ἐπιβουλεύειν ὑπώπτευσεν.

2. ἕως ἂν εἰς τὴν θάλατταν ῥέωσιν οἱ ποταμοί, οἱ ἄνθρωποι σῴζεσθαι πειράσονται.

3. (εἰ γὰρ) ἀποθάνοιμι πρὶν τοιοῦτό τι γενέσθαι.

4. τοὺς τοῦ χειμῶνος πλέοντας εὐλαβεῖσθαι δεῖ ὅπως μὴ οἱ ἄνεμοι αὐτοὺς ἐξαπατήσουσιν or ἐξαπατῶσιν.

5. οὐκ εἴα ὁ Φίλιππος τοὺς πρέσβεις οἳ ἀπαντᾶν πρὶν οἱ φίλοι αὐτοῦ τὰ τῆς πόλεως πράγματα διαφθείρειαν.

III.

(1) πρὸς ταῦτα ἀναστὰς Ξενοφῶν ὑπὲρ τῶν στρατιωτῶν εἶπεν· (2) ἡμεῖς, ὦ ἄνδρες πρέσβεις, ἥκομεν χαλεπῶς (or μόγις) τὰ σώματα καὶ τὰ ὅπλα σωσάμενοι. (3) οὐ γὰρ ἦν δυνατὸν ἅμα τὰ χρήματα φέρειν καὶ τοῖς πολεμίοις μάχεσθαι. (4) καὶ ὅποι ἂν ἐλθόντες ἀγορὰν μὴ ἔχωμεν, λαμβάνομεν τὰ ἐπιτήδεια οὐχ ὕβρει ἀλλὰ ἀνάγκῃ.

IV.

So then, Zeus, becoming afraid for our race, lest it be entirely destroyed, sends Hermes bringing a sense of shame and justice to mankind, in order that there might be organizations of cities and unifying bonds of friendship. So Hermes asks Zeus in what manner he was to give justice and shame to mankind: "As the crafts have been apportioned, so too am I to distribute these (qualities)? And the crafts have been apportioned as follows: one man having the physician's skill is sufficient to serve many laymen, and (likewise) the other craftsmen (serve many). Am I to place justice and shame too in this way in men, or am I to distribute them to all?" "To all," said Zeus, "and let all have a share. For cities would not come into being if only a few should partake of them as they do of other crafts. And establish a *law* on my authority that they put to death as a source of disease of the city anyone who is unable to have a share of shame and justice." In this way, then, Socrates, and for these reasons both other men and the Athenians believe that a few men have a share of deliberation whenever the discussion is about excellence in building and any other excellence related to a craft, and if anyone outside of the few (experts) gives advice, they do not put up with it, as you say—(and people do so) reasonably, as I say—but when they enter into debate over political excellence, which must entirely involve righteousness and self-control, reasonably they are willing to listen to every man, in the belief that it is fitting for every man to have a share of *this* virtue or else that there be no cities.

UNIT FORTY-TWO

I.

1. 1 pl. pluperf. (2) act. ind. of δέδοικα *or* δέδια
2. 3 pl. pluperf. (2) act. ind. of ἀφίστημι
3. nom. *or* voc. pl. m. perf. act. part. of τρέφω
4. fut. mid. inf. of τυγχάνω
5. 1 s. aor. pass. opt. of φαίνω
6. perf. m./p. inf. of ζεύγνυμι
7. 3 s. pres. act. opt. of ἐρωτάω
8. 3 pl. fut. mid. ind. of τρέχω
9. 2 pl. aor. act. impt. of σιγάω
10. pres. act. inf. of ὠφελέω
11. aor. act. inf. of ὀφείλω
12. 3 pl. (neut.) perf. m./p. subj. of τελευτάω
13. 2 s. aor. act. impt. of ἐλέγχω
14. nom. s. m. verbal in -τέος of φυλάττω
15. 2 s. aor. act. impt. of συγγιγνώσκω
16. perf. act. inf. of ὄμνυμι
17. 1 s. pluperf. act. ind. of παύω
18. dat. pl. m. *or* n. aor. pass. part. of πορεύω
19. perf. m./p. inf. of νικάω
20. 2 pl. perf. act. subj. of οἶδα
21. 2 s. pres. m./p. ind. *or* subj. of διανοέομαι

II.

1. ὀργίζωνται
2. ὀμνύναι
3. μεμισηκότων
4. κλαπῆς
5. καταλελείμμεθα
6. ζεύξαντα
7. ἐπιδεικνύῃ
8. διωχθήσεσθαι
9. διδαχθησομένας
10. διαβληθεῖτε or διαβληθείητε
11. ἀποστήσομαι
12. ἠγνόηντο

III.

1. (Cf. Xen. *Anab.* 4.5.1.) And on the next day it was decided that they ought to proceed as quickly as they could before the army gathered together again and captured the narrow places.
2. (Cf. Isocr. 5.81.) And do not be surprised—just as [literally, *exactly the same things that*] I wrote also to Dionysius when he acquired his tyranny—if, though being neither a general nor a politician, I have spoken to you more boldly than others do.
3. (Cf. Thuc. 1.48.1–2.) And when these preparations had been made by the Corinthians (*or* were in place for the Corinthians), taking with them three days' supply of food they went to sea during the night as if for battle, and sailing at daybreak [literally, *at the same time as dawn*] they see the ships of the Corcyraeans sailing toward them.

IV.

(1) καὶ νῦν ἐπεὶ εἰς τὰς Ἑλληνικὰς πόλεις ἤλθομεν, ἐν μὲν ἐκείνῃ (παρεῖχον γὰρ ἡμῖν ἀγοράν) εἴχομεν τὰ ἐπιτήδεια, καὶ ἀνθ᾽ ὧν ἐτίμησαν ἡμᾶς ὠφελοῦμεν αὐτούς. (2) τοὺς δὲ πολεμίους αὐτῶν ἐφ᾽ οὓς αὐτοὶ ἡγοῖντο κακῶς ἐποιοῦμεν ὅσον ἐδυνάμεθα. (3) οὗτοι δέ, οὓς ὑμετέρους φατὲ εἶναι, εἴ τι αὐτῶν εἰλήφαμεν, αὐτοὶ αἴτιοί εἰσιν· (4) οὐ γὰρ φίλιοι ἡμῖν ἦσαν, οὔτε εἴσω ἡμᾶς δεχόμενοι οὔτε ἔξω ἀγορὰν πέμποντες.

V.

Thucydides of Athens composed (this account of) the war of the Peloponnesians and Athenians, how they waged war against each other, having made his beginning immediately when the war was starting and having expected that it would be great and most noteworthy in comparison with those that occurred earlier, and judging that both sides entered it in prime condition of all military preparedness and seeing that the rest of the Greek world was taking sides with each party, some Greeks right at the start, and others in fact intending to. For this unrest turned out to be extremely significant for the Greeks and for some part of the non-Greeks, and, so to speak, even (extended) to reach a very great portion of mankind. For the events before these and the events even more ancient it was impossible* to discover reliably because of the great passage of time, but from the indications that it comes about that I trust when I investigate to the greatest possible extent, I do not believe that they [i.e., the earlier events] were great either in connection with the wars or in other respects. For it is clear that the land now called Hellas has not been firmly settled from long ago, but clearly there were migrations previously and each group easily used to leave its own territory when forced out by some group that was on each occasion more numerous.

* I follow Classen and Steup (who cite parallels) in interpreting ἀδύνατα ἦν as an archaic use of the neuter plural where other Attic prose authors would use singular ἀδύνατον ἦν: thus the subject is εὑρεῖν, the object of which is τὰ . . . παλαίτερα: see *Thukydides, erklärt von J. Classen*, Bd. 1, 4. Aufl., bearbetiet von J. Steup (Berlin 1897). Some instead treat τὰ . . . παλαίτερα as nominative subject and εὑρεῖν as epexegetic infinitive.

457898UK00009B/261

UKHW050147260425
Pitfield, Milton Keynes, MK11 3LW, UK
Ingram Content Group UK Ltd.
www.ingramcontent.com/pod-product-compliance